CASES IN

HUMAN RESOURCE MANAGEMENT

SAGE was founded in 1965 by Sara Miller McCune to support the dissemination of usable knowledge by publishing innovative and high-quality research and teaching content. Today, we publish over 900 journals, including those of more than 400 learned societies, more than 800 new books per year, and a growing range of library products including archives, data, case studies, reports, and video. SAGE remains majority-owned by our founder, and after Sara's lifetime will become owned by a charitable trust that secures our continued independence.

Los Angeles | London | New Delhi | Singapore | Washington DC | Melbourne

CASES IN
HUMAN RESOURCE MANAGEMENT

DAVID KIMBALL
Elms College

Los Angeles | London | New Delhi
Singapore | Washington DC | Melbourne

FOR INFORMATION:

SAGE Publications, Inc.
2455 Teller Road
Thousand Oaks, California 91320
E-mail: order@sagepub.com

SAGE Publications Ltd.
1 Oliver's Yard
55 City Road
London, EC1Y 1SP
United Kingdom

SAGE Publications India Pvt. Ltd.
B 1/I 1 Mohan Cooperative Industrial Area
Mathura Road, New Delhi 110 044
India

SAGE Publications Asia-Pacific Pte. Ltd.
3 Church Street
#10-04 Samsung Hub
Singapore 049483

Acquisitions Editor: Maggie Stanley
eLearning Editor: Katie Ancheta
Editorial Assistant: Neda Dallal
Production Editor: Jane Haenel
Copy Editor: Elizabeth Swearngin
Typesetter: C&M Digitals (P) Ltd.
Proofreader: Caryne Brown
Cover Designer: Janet Kiesel
Marketing Manager: Ashlee Blunk

Printed in the United States of America

Library of Congress Cataloging-in-Publication Data

Names: Kimball, David Charles, 1959- author.

Title: Cases in human resource management / by David Kimball.

Description: Los Angeles : SAGE, [2017] Identifiers: LCCN 2015045996 | ISBN 9781506332147 (pbk. : alk. paper)

Subjects: LCSH: Personnel management—Case studies.

Classification: LCC HF5549 .K4896 2016 | DDC 658.3—dc23
LC record available at http://lccn.loc.gov/2015045996

This book is printed on acid-free paper.

SUSTAINABLE FORESTRY INITIATIVE
Certified Chain of Custody
Promoting Sustainable Forestry
www.sfiprogram.org
SFI-01268

SFI label applies to text stock

16 17 18 19 20 10 9 8 7 6 5 4 3 2 1

• Brief Contents •

• Detailed Contents •

• Foreword •

The current buzzword in both business and academia is *engaged*. Today's millennial students don't want to simply be lectured at; they want to be actively engaged in their learning, and they want relevant real-world businesses examples. The AACSB (Association to Advance Collegiate Schools of Business) accrediation standards clearly state the importance of decision-making skills.

Over the years, trends have come and gone, but the case method of developing decision-making skills through the use of case studies of real-world organizations has passed the test of time to become the classic teaching method. Case studies require the student to think critically in analyzing information and in making decisions.

David Kimball's *Cases in Human Resource Management* offers real-world business cases to meet the millennial students' need to be engaged, and they can be used to meet the AACSB standard of developing the important decision-making skill. Kimball has selected a good variety of organizations. Some of the popular businesses that students want to learn more about include Zappos, LinkedIn, Costco, Walmart, GE, Hilton, and Visier.

Kimball's *Cases in Human Resource Management* is a good supplement, not only to the HRM course, but also for most organizational behavior and management books, and I recommend it.

Robert N. Lussier
Professor of Management
Springfield College

• Preface •

This casebook is designed using the five parts of *Human Resource Management: Functions, Applications, and Skills Development*, Second Edition, by Robert N. Lussier and John R. Hendon. Each case is about a thousand words, which allows the student to learn about the company, people, and the human resource issue within each case. However, students are encouraged to use the *Human Resource Management* textbook by Lussier and Hendon to learn more about the human resource issue within the case.

Part I: 21st-Century Human Resource Management Strategic Planning and Legal Issues

In Chapter 1, a case about Zappos helps set up a more modern way to look at employees as human resources—with an emphasis on human. The second case reviews the five growing areas where a student might work in a human resources department. Students need to learn what these five growing areas are so they can explore them throughout the casebook.

Chapter 2 starts with a case that requires the student to determine the viability of an early retirement offer in the state of Massachusetts. The second case investigates how Costco develops happy employees.

Chapter 3 is about a very recent trend where companies, such as Walmart, are offering more than the required minimum wage. The second case is about diversity and affirmative action at Hilton Hotels.

Part II: Staffing

Chapter 4 explores Visier and the services it provides HR departments by helping to forecast workforce needs. The second case looks back at the famous succession planning process that Jack Welch used to select his own replacement as chief executive officer at General Electric (GE).

The cases in Chapter 5 explore e-recruitment and having to make a decision to hire an internal employee or an external candidate to fill an open position.

The first case in Chapter 6 uses the author's own experiences of recruiting and selecting a new college professor. The second case is about an employee, "Walter," who is rejected as being a good fit for Google.

Part III: Developing and Managing

Chapter 7 presents the latest ideas about Massive Open Online Courses (MOOCs), such as Coursera and Udacity, and their ability to recruit and train employees. The second case follows the talented Harry Saunders and his career development at the Big Buy Supermarket.

The first case in Chapter 8 is about the importance of using performance appraisals. The second case is about the problems using performance appraisal forms!

The first case in Chapter 9 is about the importance of coaching, counseling, and disciplining employees. The importance of documentation is emphasized. The second case presents the concept of mindfulness and how it can be used as a thoughtful way to lead employees.

The first case in Chapter 10 challenges management and unions to work together. The second case deals specifically with managing angry employees.

Part IV: Compensating

The first case in Chapter 11 is about how wage compression and pay secrecy affect employee motivation. The second case discusses whether employees are motivated at work based on their expectations or are treated equally.

Chapter 12 debates some of the newer issues involved in executive pay since the introduction of Sarbanes-Oxley reform in 2012 (SOX) and the Dodd-Frank Wall Street Reform and Consumer Protection Act of 2010.

Chapter 13 covers benefits and how some employers are kicking your spouse off your health-care plans to reduce benefit costs. The second case examines new laws regarding sick leave for employees.

Part V: Protecting and Expanding Organizational Reach

Chapter 14 is about building an HR information system (HRIS) while protecting health information (PHI) from cyber attacks. This is a timely issue with the increased occurrence in cyber theft in all industries. The second case starts to wrap up the book by discussing future trends in human resources.

Chapter 15 explores whether HR can help companies develop corporate social responsibility (CSR) programs. The second case examines equal opportunity, diversity, and how five generations of people are at work together. Professors and readers might find the case on five generations of people at work together as the most interesting case in the book.

Chapter 16 concludes the book with cases related to people the author knows (names have been changed) who have worked in various countries in their careers. The first case discusses the role of a marketing director living in England. The second case asks readers to put themselves in the shoes of a young Russian lady who comes to the United States and finds that her language and math skills are very valuable in the workplace.

The author welcomes comments about individual cases at kimballd@elms.edu. Readers are also welcome to send updated material they find regarding each case. Ideas for new cases are also greatly welcome.

David Kimball

Teaching notes for the case studies in the book are available to instructors at **study.sagepub.com/kimball.**

• Acknowledgments •

This casebook would not have been possible without the support of my family: Amy, Carly, and Jacob. I appreciate the guidance of Dr. Robert Lussier, whose textbook was the inspiration for this casebook. I would also like to thank Maggie Stanley and Neda Dallal from SAGE Publishing, who helped organize all the cases.

SAGE Publishing gratefully acknowledges the following reviewers:

Ralph Braithwaite, *University of Hartford*

Leslie Campbell, *Colby-Sawyer University*

Joseph M. Goodman, *Illinois State University*

Gundars Kaupins, *Boise State University*

Claire Kent, *Mary Baldwin College*

Ernest Kovacs, *Fairleigh Dickinson University*

Kim Lukaszewski, *Wright State University*

Carl Maertz, *Saint Louis University*

Dan Morrell, *Middle Tennessee State University*

Lisa O'Hara, *Pennsylvania State University*

Kern Peng, *Santa Clara University*

Matthew Stollak, *St. Norbert College*

Mussie Tessema, *Winona State University*

Thomas R. Tudor, *University of Arkansas at Little Rock*

• About the Author •

David Kimball, PhD, has been professor of management at Elms College in Chicopee, Massachusetts, for nearly three decades. He is the chair of the Division of Business, which includes majors in accounting, management, marketing, sport management, and health care management. Professor Kimball has taught business strategy and global ethics courses at the undergraduate and MBA levels. Dr. Kimball has co-authored a textbook on sports management and a new book on entrepreneurship.

As a former employee at the old AT&T, he is often interested in the mobile communications industry and the technology used in similar industries. Before entering the field of teaching on a full-time basis, Dr. Kimball worked at Mass Mutual Life Insurance Company as a corporate trainer. At times, Dr. Kimball's early work experiences at McDonald's can be found in his views since he still believes in the McDonald's credo of cleanliness, service, and value. Dr. Kimball completed his dissertation on the topic of business mission and written mission statements while finishing his doctorate degree in management systems.

21st-CENTURY HUMAN RESOURCE MANAGEMENT STRATEGIC PLANNING AND LEGAL ISSUES

The New Human Resource Management Process

Case 1.1. The Changing Role of Human Resources in Organizations: The Curious Case of Zappos

In the 1980s, when you were interviewed or hired for a job you often met a person from the company who worked in the Personnel Office. The Personnel Office was viewed as a place where each employee filed the necessary forms to work at the company.

The Personnel Office was considered a *staff management area* where you learned about the policies and rules of being an employee at the company. Personnel was considered a *staff management area*, since they only advised line managers in some field of expertise. For example, Personnel would have consultants with specialized experience in accounting or providing input on legal issues to support the line managers that were creating the product.

Fortunately, over the years the Personnel Office became known as the Human Resources (HR) Department. HR has become a larger part of the strategic planning process in many companies. The HR manager often helps to set policies and strategies in relation to the workforce at an organization. At the same time, HR managers continue to support line managers by constantly improving areas such as finding prospective new employees, training employees, improving employee motivation, searching and evaluating lower cost and higher quality health-care benefits, providing information on retirement services, and many other activities designed to make sure employees are able to complete their jobs.

Zappos, a very successful online retailer that sells shoes mainly to women, is an example of a younger company that provides a modern approach to human resource management. The human resources department at Zappos organizes unique events to help celebrate the excitement at Zappos. To begin the process of working at Zappos, the initial job interview is often conducted in an informal atmosphere to allow the prospective employee to feel comfortable. New employees are offered $2,000 if they don't want to stay with the company. Very few employees decide to leave the company since they are excited to work for Zappos and their exciting CEO Tony Heish.[1]

Zappos has been so successful that it was purchased by Amazon in 2009 for over $807 million. Zappos runs independently of Amazon to protect its unique human resources department.[2]

Rebecca Henry is the former director of human resources for Zappos. She believes the company consciously decides what the corporate culture needs to look like based on ten core values. Each new employee is trained by an HR person on each of the following ten values:

1. Deliver WOW Through Service

2. Embrace and Drive Change

3. Create Fun and a Little Weirdness

4. Be Adventurous

5. Be Creative and Open-Minded

6. Pursue Growth and Learning

7. Build Open and Honest Relationships With Communication

8. Build a Positive Team and Family Spirit

9. Do More With Less

10. Be Passionate and Determined, Be Humble[3]

The HR Department works with upper-level management to develop employee job descriptions, the hiring process, on-the-job training, and the day-to-day work environment based on these unique core values.

Zappos is always exploring new ideas to improve its human resources process. For example, to improve the recruiting process, it has developed a social network known as Zappos Insiders. Zappos Insiders allows prospective employees to interact with current employees to see if they would be a good fit with the creative culture at Zappos.[4]

Tony Heish's latest idea is to make sure the people working at Zappos are truly motivated to work at his company. All employees were offered the option to leave the company with a severance package if they didn't want to participate in a self-management program. *Self-management* is a newer management idea that is based on having agile workers. Employees learn to manage themselves and move from job to job instead of staying with a single static job. The goal is for employees to give up traditional job titles and work on multiple tasks, rather than at a specific job. An employee's job is constantly changing instead of being static.

Overall, 220 employees (14%) took the severance package offered by Heish to weed out employees who wanted to change companies, who were ready for retirement, or decided to leave for their own reasons. However, that also means 84 percent of the remaining employees are employees who are motivated to make Zappos an even more successful online retailer.[5]

Case Questions

1. Should Tony Heish be concerned that a large number of managers and employees might reject self-management, leave the company, and accept a severance package?

2. What benefits or incentives do employees experience at Zappos that make them want to stay with the company?

3. Does it appear the Human Resources Department at Zappos is a staff or a line area?

4. Does human resources at Zappos create revenue for the organization?

5. If you were the HR manager at Zappos, would you support the Zappos Insider program as a reliable source of acquiring new prospective employees?

Case 1.2. HRM Careers:
Five Growing Areas of Human Resources

What does it mean if you say you want to work in human resources? Actually, if you can show a desire to work in HR, that is great! Too many students lack a focus on what they specifically want to do for a job and a career. So, being able to say one wants to work in HR shows that a student has scoped out an area he or she would like to learn more about and gain experience in.

A person who would like to work in human resources can expect to work closely with the other people in the organization. Thus, an HR employee needs to have good people skills, as the HR job will be to take the lead in the management and maintenance of the organization's people. The HR person might find his or her job to be as delightful as helping employees who have a new baby in their family or as sad as helping with employees who leave the company, are laid off from the company, or even pass away.

Human Resources employees are increasingly asked to see the big picture of the organization. They need to know where the company is going so they can hire the appropriate people to fill those positions. For example, if a supermarket chain decided to add gasoline stations to its stores, then the company might need to hire a person who had experience in gasoline sales instead of—or along with—knowledge of food sales.

The Bureau of Labor Statistics (BLS.gov) provides data on human resource management jobs for the 2012 to 2022 range. Median pay in the field of human resources is expected to be just under $100,000 per year, or $47.94 per hour. The data are based on a person having a bachelor's degree and 5 years of related work experience. Job growth over the 10-year period is expected to be 13 percent, which is considered as fast as the average growth in all occupations. The average job rate in all occupations is expected to be 11 percent.[6]

HR jobs can be classified as either generalist or specialist. An HR *generalist* may operate in many different areas of the discipline. A *specialist* focuses on a specific discipline of HR. Many smaller organizations have only one or two employees in their HR office. The HR employees will have to be generalists inasmuch as they will have to help employees in many different areas.

The following are the human resources positions that are expected to grow in the next five years:

1. *Compensation and Benefits Managers.* The Bureau of Labor Statistics (BLS.gov) explains that these managers plan, direct, and coordinate how much an organization pays its employees and how employees are paid. Benefits managers plan, direct, and coordinate retirement plans, health insurance, and other benefits that an organization offers its employees. For example, employees can select a health-care plan for their family from the benefit manager. Employees will then periodically ask questions about their plan throughout the year. The benefits manager will end up answering questions regarding the deductible level in the plan, which the family must pay before most medical services are free. One plan, for example, may have a $4,000 deductible. That amount of medical care money must be spent before services are reimbursed. Employees can also ask the benefits expert for help with purchasing medical supplies via mail order instead of using a local pharmacist. Salaries can range from $48,000 to $98,000, depending on where you live.

2. *Training and Development Specialists.* The median wage for trainers was $56,000 in 2012. Training and development is the area of the company where employees receive education. Trainers need to have good communication skills, as they lead training sessions on topics such as leadership, teamwork, and product-specific information.[7]

3. *Employment, Recruitment, and Staffing Specialists.* These HR workers are employment specialists who screen, recruit, interview, and place workers. The goal of staffing specialists is to get talented people interested in working for their company. Mean wages are around $63,000 a year.

4. *Human Resources Information (HRIS) Analysts.* This person uses computer skills to help ensure the data within the human resources department. They ensure the integrity of the data, testing of system changes, and analysis of data flows for process improvement.

5. *Employee Assistance Plan (EAP) Managers.* Many small to large businesses have an EAP program to help employees with their personal health. EAPs can include counseling for work-related stress, financial problems, and substance-abuse problems. Wellness programs can include assistance with weight problems and encourage physical fitness programs.

Case Questions

1. Which of the previous positions listed deals with problems you might have regarding your health-care program?

2. Which positions would be well suited to someone who likes to make presentations?

3. A person with computer skills would be best suited for which position?

4. A person with social worker experience would be well suited to which type of position?

5. A person who would find, attract, and assign people to a certain division would have which job title?

Notes

1. McFarland, Keith, "Why Zappos Offers New Hires $2,000 to Quit," *Bloomberg Business,* September 16, 2008.
2. Hof, Rob, "Amazon.com Acquires Shoe E-tailer Zappos," *BusinessWeek*, July 22, 2009.
3. Heathfield, Susan M., "20 Ways Zappos Reinforces Its Company Culture," Humanresources.com.
4. Feffer, Mark, "The Democratization of Talent Management: How Technology and Generational Changes Are Transforming HR," *Society for Human Resource Management*, April 7, 2015.
5. Feloni, Richard, "7% of Zappos Managers Quit After Recent CEO Ultimatum to Embrace Self-Management or Leave," *Businessinsider.com*, June 9, 2015.
6. http://www.bls.gov/ooh/management/human-resources-managers.htm.
7. http://www.bls.gov/ooh/business-and-financial/training-and-development-specialists.htm.

2

Strategy-Driven Human Resource Management

Case 2.1. The External Environment: When State Government Offers Early Retirement

The *external environment* consists of a series of influences that originate outside the organization and that the company cannot control. These external factors, which must be considered when forming a strategy, include customers, competition, suppliers, shareholders, society, technology, the economy, the labor force, and our government.

In regard to the external force of the government, we have come to expect our government agencies to be complex, formalized, and centralized in terms of organizational structure.

Government agencies are very large organizations that are normally very complex. *Complexity* involves the way in which we divide the organization into different segments. Government agencies are often organized into many different layers of employees, which makes communication more difficult between the different parts of the agency. Government agencies are often known to be very slow at making decisions.

Government jobs are often standardized (*formalization*) within an agency, since they have to make decisions based upon many policies, procedures, and rules. Although these rules help employees to make routine decisions, they also stifle creativity since employees must also follow these rules.

Overall, government agency decision making needs to be made by top government officials (*centralization*) to ensure the same decision is given to each citizen. Centralization helps to maintain control and should also result in lower costs.

National, state, and local governments all set laws and regulations that businesses must obey. Federal and state governments create opportunities and obstacles for businesses. Safety standards set by government agencies, such as the Occupational Safety and Health Administration (OSHA), are meant to increase employee safety while in a working environment. The Environmental Protection Agency (EPA) set standards to reduce pollution. Although it can be expensive for a company to meet the standards of these types of agencies, the laws are designed to improve our quality of life at work and at home.

However, just like a for-profit company, the government has to be careful about hiring people to work in its agencies. At times, the government can experience a deficit and has to entice its employees to accept an early retirement program.

In Massachusetts, the state government had a primary goal of achieving budget savings of $172 million by offering an early retirement incentive package. Governor Charlie Baker and his people estimated that 4,500 state workers would take the incentive. The actual number of people who applied for retirement was about 2,870.[1] The reduced number of employees who accepted the reduced early retirement program might result in layoffs in state employees. However, the governor has promised to look for other solutions besides layoffs.

The state wanted to use 20 percent of the savings to refill positions that were now open. As an extra incentive, the state offered a $10,000 buyout to employees who were eligible to retire. It appears that 100 fully ready to retire employees accepted the extra $10,000 offer.[2]

The state of Massachusetts's forecast for how many employees would take the early retirement package should have considered multiple issues. For example, Massachusetts had a record snowfall of 100 inches in the winter of 2015. The increased amount of snowfall should have enticed more government employees to retire early so they could move to a warmer climate. However, the people of Massachusetts are used to snowy winters—fewer left the state, or their position with the government, than expected.

Employees also are more likely to accept an early retirement program if they have been preparing for their own retirement. If employees have saved money in preparation for their retirement, then they would be able to retire early since they will have enough money in retirement. But employees who have not saved enough for their retirement will need to continue to work to receive their salary.

Last, employees can have social reasons for working toward their proper retirement age of approximately 66 years old. Many employees enjoy the job they do at work. The job gives them motivation to wake up in the morning, to achieve something at work that is meaningful and can help other people, they enjoy their salary level and benefits package, and they enjoy the friendships of the fellow workers.

Enticing your employees to retire early from the company (or government) is lined with many potential problems. Here are a few examples:

- A "brain drain" situation can occur if your best and most important employees take the early retirement package. Key knowledge toward running the operation will be lost if your experienced employees decide to leave the organization early.
- A serious lack of talent can also happen if the number of people taking the early retirement package is more than expected.
- There would be fewer employees left to deal with the face-to-face interactions with customers if the middle-to-lower level state employees decided to take the early retirement package.
- It will cost more money up front to entice people to want to retire early.

Case Questions

1. Which force of the external environment has the greatest impact on the state of Massachusetts?

2. Which force would you select as the second greatest impact on the state?

3. Should the state be concerned if more than 4,500 employees elected to retire?

4. In regard to structure, how would you consider the state with respect to complexity, formalization, and centralization?

5. If you were an employee of Zappos or the state of Massachusetts, would you take early retirement? Assume you qualify for the extra $10,000 incentive. You are currently 58 years old.

Case 2.2. HR Strategy: Employees Matter at Costco

Costco is a wholesaler and a retailer—customers love to shop at Costco and buy consumer goods in bulk packages. At the same time, the employees who work at Costco are equally happy with their jobs at Costco. No wonder the company is ranked in the 2015 top 100 workforces.[3]

Organizational culture consists of the values, beliefs, and assumptions about appropriate behavior that members of an organization share. The former CEO at Costco, Jim Sinegal, said, "When employees are happy, they are your very best ambassadors."[4] Although many companies say employees are their most important asset, there is a special emphasis on employees at Costco. Sinegal is considered a hero at Costco because he started out his career a bag boy, worked his way up to VP of merchandising and operations, and eventually co-founded Costco in 1983.

There are plenty of stories of people buying a Costco rotisserie chicken for $4.99 and having no idea why Costco keeps the price so low. The price of a hot dog and soda for $1.50 hasn't changed since the mid-1980s. However, the $1.50 price is a symbol of how much Costco cares about its customers; it keeps its price low so that customers, who often drive quite far to reach a Costco store, have very affordable options to eat while shopping at the store.[5]

Employees at Costco are also treated extremely well. Costco pays its employees much higher than the minimum wage. The company also pays about 90 percent of health-care benefits for full and part-time workers. There is a clear path provided for employees to grow and develop with the company.

Competitive advantage (CA) is a key strategic topic often associated with Professor Michael Porter from Harvard.[6] *Competitive advantage* is the area of an organization that is unique and keeps an organization ahead of its competitors. Determining the competitive advantage for an organization is the job of management leaders. In the case of Costco, competitive advantage lies in the ability to sell bulk packages of food items at a lower cost per unit than traditional supermarkets. Of course, these food items (along with nonfood items such as clothes, books, and videos) are stocked and sold by extremely pleasant and helpful employees. The key to a competitive advantage is to make sure it is a sustainable competitive advantage (SCA). An *SCA* would mean the advantage the company has is not easily copied, outdated due to new innovations or technology, or in general no longer having a valid competitive advantage.

With the goal of a SCA in mind, Porter also developed his *Five-Force Model of Competition.*[7] Porter's five forces are Supplier Power, Buyer Power, Threat of New Entry, Threat of Substitution, and Competitive Rivalry. In Costco's case, Costco is such a large retailer that it can buy large amounts of products, such as Coca-Cola and Oreo cookies, that it can get items at the lowest possible cost. Plus, Costco has its own brand name, Kirkland, which also increases its control over suppliers. In regard to substitutions, there is really no replacement for food. However, the force of a Threat of New Entrants is quite possible. For example, Amazon is the largest retailer online and recently surpassed Walmart as the largest company in market value. Costco has to be concerned that its customers will increasingly buy their food items online at Amazon instead of going out to shop at a Costco store.

As one can see, in many industries, the competitive rivalry within an industry is as great as at any time in the history of business. Thus, Costco will have to emphasize its great face-to-face customer service offered at all of its stores. It certainly helps to have pleasant people at their doors checking customers into and out of the store. Of course, that is also a security check to make sure customers have their membership on the way into the store and that they have a receipt for buying the products on the way out of the store.

Based on personal experiences since 1991, the author's family has bought grocery and nongrocery items at Costco. We are loyal customers, and the employees are always sincerely helpful 100 percent of the time. The level of service, including returning any product that has ever been bought at Costco, is not found at any other retailer. Costco's focus on employee happiness translates to customer satisfaction. Happy employees make happy customers.

Case Questions

1. Costco has impacted the retail shopping industry. Use the Five-Force model to outline how Costco impacted the grocery and nongrocery marketplace.

2. How does Costco's approach to human resources provide it with a competitive advantage?

3. How do Costco's HR policies help the company be successful?

4. Discuss how Costco creates a link between employees and customers.

5. Does the mission of Costco impact HR?

Notes

1. Associated Press, "Early Retirement Signups for Massachusetts State Workers Below Projections as Deadline Nears," FoxBusiness.com, June 12, 2015.

2. Schoenberg, Shira, "2,870 Sign Up for Early Retirement," *The Republican,* June 13, 2015, 1.

3. "2015 Workforce 100: Ranking the World's Top Companies for HR," *Workforce,* May 22, 2015, http://www.workforce.com/articles/21293–2015-Workforce-100-List.

4. "Employee Relations Best Practices: Costco's Approach to HR," *i-Sight,* http://i-sight.com/resources/employee-relations-best-practices-costco/.

5. Tuttle, Brad, "Why Costco May Never Raise Prices on $4.99 Chickens, $1.50 Hot Dogs," *Time.com,* May 29, 2015.

6. Porter, Michael, "Competitive Advantage," *Free Press,* 1998.

7. Airline, Katherine, "Porter's Five Forces: Analyzing the Competition," Businessnewsdaily.com, February 18, 2015, http://www.businessnewsdaily.com/5446-porters-five-forces.html.

3

The Legal Environment and Diversity Management

Case 3.1. Major Employment Laws: How Does an Increase in State Minimum Wage Impact an Organization?

In any management position, you need a basic understanding of the major employment laws. If you are the manager of a company, such as Walmart, you have to understand what is legal and what isn't, or you may cost your employer money.

There are some laws that deal specifically with compensation issues. A major piece of legislation was the Equal Pay Act of 1963, which requires that women be paid equal to men if they are doing the same work. However, the oldest of the compensation laws is the Fair Labor Standards Act (FLSA) of 1938. The FLSA covers minimum wages, overtime issues, and child labor issues within the United States.

The federal minimum wage set by FLSA is currently $7.25 per hour. States cannot set a minimum wage that is lower than the federal standard, but they are free to establish a higher one. The minimum rate in different states can be found at The National Conference of State Legislators.[1]

President Obama has made increasing the minimum wage a priority during his presidency. He believes that low minimum wages create "social inequality." He has called for a minimum of at least $10.10 per hour.[2] Even still, there is little doubt this increase will not be enough to help low-income people escape poverty. But it would be progress, and it would help low-income people earn more money.

Employees, especially in the fast-food industry, have been holding rallies across the nation to increase the minimum wage. The rallying cry has been for $15.00 per hour for a minimum wage. This is a fight for everyone who is paid minimum wage, not just the fast-food industry.

For example, the city of Los Angeles voted in 2015 to increase its minimum wage from $9 per hour to $15 per hour by 2020. The minimum wage rate will be $10 in California in 2016 and $13.00 in 2017.[3] More large cities are expected to follow.

In New York, Governor Andrew Cuomo is siding with the minimum wage earners. Cuomo rallied against McDonald's and Burger King, where pay is so low that employees are forced to accept state assistance.[4]

Walmart has been at the center of the minimum wage rate for many years. Since Walmart is the largest physical retailer in the world, it should have expected its wage rate would be scrutinized by all the stakeholders of the organization.

In response, Walmart has increased its minimum salary to $9 per hour, which will bump up to $10 by February 2016. Around 500,000 employees will receive the hourly increase. It is hoped that the increases can help many Walmart employees who are on state assistance. Walmart didn't decide to suddenly be kind to its employees. Since most states now have a rate higher than the federal minimum rate, Walmart made the change because it was going to legally have to pay its employees the higher rate in different states.

Human resources departments need to be prepared for the increase in minimum wages. HR needs to understand its own business situation and build a business model that will include higher minimum wages. Some companies, such as Costco, Ikea, and The Gap already pay their workers above the federal minimum wage.[5]

HR also has to be concerned about wage compression between hourly employees and supervisors. If the minimum rate rises high enough, the hourly workers could be paid as high as, or even higher than, their supervisors and managers. This could cause problems with employees, since they might rather be an hourly worker than of a salaried employee.

The success of the rallies, the increase in state and local wages, and the decision by large companies to increase their minimum wage is certainly positive news for the lives of many Americans. But it is most likely that employers are also going to decide to hire fewer employees since they will claim it is too expensive to hire the same number of minimum wage employees as they currently hire. Consequently, it is possible that low-income, entry-level employees will have fewer job opportunities because employers will try to reduce the number of employees they hire.

Case Questions

1. What law(s) apply to this case?

2. Will Walmart employ fewer minimum wage employees to save money?

3. Will low-income employees need more education and skills?

4. Will more college-educated prospective employees be offered jobs at $15 per hour instead of a salaried position?

5. What is your view on the increase in the minimum wage? How has it affected yourself at your own job?

Case 3.2. Diversity and Inclusion: What's the Difference?

Hilton Worldwide Named Top 50 Diversity Company

Diversity and inclusion are important concepts in ensuring that all human beings in your organization are treated equally. Companies have learned that their employees should represent their customers. All companies sell their products and services to an increasingly diverse population. Thus, the employee makeup of the firm should also be diverse.

Diversity refers to all the ways we differ. Anything that makes us unique is part of diversity. Inclusion involves bringing together and harnessing these diverse forces and resources in a way that is beneficial.[6] An organization needs to be aware of the diverse nature of their organization, then create programs to help include all the diverse groups to feel comfortable, wanted, and motivated to work for the company.

Diversity is important and needed because, as the white population continues to shrink and the minority population grows, selling your product to a variety of groups increases sales, revenues, and profits. Embracing diversity means you will create new business opportunities by having employees who look at the world from different perspectives.

Human resources needs to be fully trained and aware of all the laws related to the topic as applied in organizations. Thus, Title VII of the Civil Rights Act of 1964, the Americans with Disabilities Act of 1990, the Age Discrimination Employment Act of 1967, and other laws need to be fully understood and implemented by HR employees. HR should be involved in training employees to foster diversity and to be accepting of ideas created by each group. HR can be the facilitator to help the organization stay within the laws of discrimination and, at the same time, help foster a better understanding between employees from different backgrounds.

Hilton Worldwide was selected as DiversityInc's Top 50 Companies for Diversity.[7] Based upon DiversityInc's research, the top 50 companies have 20 percent more Blacks, Latinos, and Asians in management, and 13 percent more women.

Here are some reasons that Hilton Worldwide was selected as an above average diversity company:

- "Diversity and inclusion are part of our DNA at Hilton," said Christopher J. Nassetta, president and CEO of Hilton Worldwide. "Like our hotels, our workforce is global, and our success is driven by the passion and motivation of our teams. Our culture and diversity in all its forms around the world makes our organization strong and drives better results."[8]
- Hilton Worldwide supports the LGBT community by participating in two of the nation's largest Pride festivals.

- Hilton has a National Minority Supplier Development Council Board of Directors. Their goal is to help influence the development of Asian, Black, Hispanic, and Native American suppliers and supplier diversity best practices.
- Hilton Worldwide was ranked on the Hispanic Business 2012 Best Companies for Diversity list by *Hispanic Business* magazine. Hilton scored among the highest in restaurants and resorts.
- Hilton Worldwide offers excellent employee resource groups, including a group for veterans and their spouses.

How does Hilton Worldwide do in passing the OUCH test? The OUCH test, although not a legal test, is a good theory and rule of thumb as to what makes a fair human resource decision. OUCH is an acronym for a decision that is *objective, uniform in application, consistent in effect*, and *related to the job*.[9] The OUCH test should be used whenever considering any action that involves employees.

The "O" in OUCH means employment actions are made as objectively as possible. Objective means the HR decision is based on fact, cognitive knowledge, or quantifiable evidence in all cases. In comparison, employment actions should not be based on something that is subjective, such as your emotional state, your opinion, or how you feel in a certain situation.

The "U" in OUCH considers whether an employment action is being uniformly applied to all employment decisions. For example, if one candidate for a management position at Hilton has to take a written test as part of the job process, then you also need to have all the applicants for the position complete the written test, under the same conditions, to the best of your ability.

The "C" in OUCH considers whether the employment actions taken have significantly different effects on one or more protected groups than it has on majority group. Title VII of the Civil Rights Act of 1964 prohibits employment discrimination based on race, color, religion, sex, or national origin. Managers have to be careful they don't affect a protected group disproportionately with an employment action. It is important for managers to show consistency in their employment actions.

The "H" in OUCH determines whether the employment action directly relates to the primary aspects of the job in question. If the job of a manager at the Hilton does not include serving coffee to employees in the morning, then the manager cannot be hired or fired for not serving coffee.

On all accounts, a company like Hilton Worldwide, that is thought of as a Best Company for Diversity, passes the OUCH test. Hilton has done an excellent job of including all sorts of diverse groups (such as veterans and their spouses, Asian, Hispanic, and Black employees and suppliers, and the LGBT community) in its diversity and inclusion programs.

Case Questions

1. What laws do you think might apply in this case?

2. What is the difference between diversity and inclusion?

3. What is the role of human resources in fostering diversity?

4. Does Hilton Worldwide pass the OUCH test?

5. Discuss different groups of people/ employees that would be considered diverse.

Notes

1. National Conference of State Legislators, retrieved November 27, 2015, http://www.ncsl .org/research/labor-and-employment/state-minimum-wage-chart.aspx.

2. Sahadi, Jeanne, "Will a Higher Minimum Wage Really Reduce Income Inequality?" *CNN Money,* January 15, 2014.

3. Wattles, Jackie, "Los Angeles Is Now Largest City in America With $15 Minimum," *CNN Money,* June 14, 2015.

4. Bredderman, Will, "At Minimum Wage Rally, Cuomo Attacks Term 'Income Inequality,'" June 11, 2015, http://observer.com/2015/06/at-minimum-wage-rally-cuomo-attacks-term-income-inequality/.

5. Patton, Carol, "Employers Embracing Wage Hike," *Human Resource Executive Online,* October 13, 2014.

6. Jordan, T. Hudson, "Moving From Diversity to Inclusion," *Diversity Journal.com,* March 22, 2011.

7. "Hilton Worldwide Named One of DiversityInc's 2015 Top 50 Companies for Diversity: Hilton Also Named a Top 10 Company for Supplier Diversity," *Hilton Worldwide.com,* April 24, 2015.

8. http://news.hiltonworldwide.com/index.cfm/newsroom/category/topic/732.

9. Hendon, John, "The Ouch Test: A Tool for Managing Your Employees," *Ask the HR Department. com,* 2013.

STAFFING

Matching Employees and Jobs

Job Analysis and Design

Case 4.1. HR Forecasting:
Visier—Workforce Forecasting

For an organization to maximize productivity, HR must match the right people with the right jobs. HR forecasting identifies the estimated supply and demand for the different types of human resources needed in the organization over some future period, based on past and present demand.

Employment software specialist Visier Inc. helps companies complete their HR forecast. Visier is an employment specialist located in Vancouver, British Columbia, and San Jose, California. The company provides assistance and solutions to for improving recruitment, retaining employees, and motivating employees.

Visier takes complex data (often called Big Data) and uses Cloud technology to store and analyze workforce data. It then turns the data into sensible workforce strategies. Led by CEO John Schwarz, Visier has successfully developed HR strategies with Yahoo, Time Inc., ConAgra Foods, Nissan, and AOL.[1]

Using its special Workforce Intelligence process, Visier analyzes company data to predict which valuable employees are most likely to leave the company, provide insight into proper compensation levels, and discover recruitment sources that will result in finding the most talented recruits.

Visier predicts that companies will start to look at the overall cost of human resources, instead of just counting the number of people. Through its Workforce Intelligence process, Visier will also help predict the impact of employee retirement and how to best transfer employee skills to the next generation.

Visier has been so successful at helping companies organize their human resources they have attracted $25.5 million in new financing from investors.[2] Visier's software will bring even more big data analytical technologies to the human resources market. HR software that analyzes HR needs such as job analysis, job descriptions, job specifications, job design and redesign, job simplification, and job expansion is at least an $8 billion market.

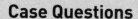

Case Questions

1. Do you agree with using an employment service such as Visier to help recruit, train, and develop your employees?

2. Do you think an outside vendor such as Visier can properly match prospective employees with open jobs?

3. Do you think Visier can complete an HR forecast for a company?

4. If you used Visier services, would you expect to lay off employees?

5. Why is forecasting retirements important in regard to the next generation of employees?

Case 4.2. Succession Planning: Developing Leaders at General Electric (GE)

Succession planning requires planning for a smooth transition from one key employee to another in order to minimize disruption of the organization's work. Even if you own your own business, you eventually have to transfer ownership to the next generation. Having a succession plan is part of forecasting the future human resource needs of a company. A well-thought-out succession plan can reduce risk within the company by making sure the company is being led by a top-notch executive. Staff morale should be increased since the person selected currently works for the company. Hiring an executive from within will show that all employees who work for the company have the potential to be promoted.

GE was highly successful under the unique leadership that former CEO Jack Welch provided. Welch was known for making brash statements to help motivate employees. In an interview in the *Los Angeles Times*, Jeff Christian, the CEO of Christian Timbers Inc., said of Welch,

> The winners are the people who make hiring and keeping the best people a top priority, and that's exactly what Jack Welch did. . . . His primary strategic goal was hiring the best people around, developing them and training them and knowing who the stars were.[3]

On the other hand, Welch could be tough on his employees. He created what was affectionately called "rank and yank." His model was that the star employees (10%) were encouraged to stay at GE. The middle 80 percent were considered the average employee with potential growth and development. Welch felt the bottom 10 percent of employees should be encouraged to leave GE. The bottom 10 percent received counseling on finding their next employer. Although the performance system was often considered harsh, Welch felt it was transparent, and an honest approach to help develop employees either at GE or another company.[4]

The classic case of succession planning took place at General Electric (GE) in 2001. At that time, Jack Welch had been the CEO at GE for 20 years. Welch had set a succession plan in place by the mid-1990s. He created a list of 23 essential skills, characteristics, and qualities a CEO should possess. He would move executives into different positions and strategic business units in an effort to cross train his leaders in all areas of the company. Jack was left with eight candidates who were all very qualified to run GE or another large corporation.

Jeff Immelt was eventually selected to succeed Welch, and he has been at the helm of GE for the last 14 years. The executives not selected were so talented they were often chosen by other large corporations to be their CEO. Bob Nardelli went from GE to CEO at Home Depot. He then went to Chrysler. Jim McNerny went from GE to CEO of 3M, and then he moved to Boeing.

Jack Welch's succession planning process is the model that many corporations have used to replace CEOs. The process Welch created led to the creation of a "deep bench" of talented executives to compete against each other in order to see who would be the next CEO. The succession plan itself helped GE to develop its top-level managers.

Welch also started the succession plan many years before he actually retired so he didn't have to rush to pick his successor. He challenged the executive candidates with "stretch assignments" to see who could thrive in increasingly difficult situations. The *stretch assignments* were projects the eight candidates were given beyond their normal skills and abilities. Stretch assignments placed the candidates into new, larger, and potentially uncomfortable projects and tasks in order to see who could learn to grow into the next CEO at GE.

In the end, the succession planning process worked for the GE's Board of Directors. They were left with a CEO, Jeff Immelt, who has successfully led GE for many years. Jack Welch retired from GE as planned and has continued to be a key speaker at conferences and training seminars about how to motivate, develop, and promote human resources.

Case Questions

1. Why do family businesses have to be as concerned as large corporations about succession planning?

2. Is succession planning part of forecasting human resources?

3. Did Jack Welch place great value on human resources at GE?

4. Why were the stretch assignments important to the selection of the new CEO at GE?

5. Find the CEO of a local company and determine how long he/she has been the CEO.

Notes

1. www.visier.com.
2. Shieber, Jonathan, "Combining Big Data and Human Resources Nets Visier $25.5 Million," *Tech Crunch.com*, June 10, 2014.
3. Girion, Lisa, "GE Succession a Leadership Lesson," *Los Angeles Times,* December 3, 2000.
4. Welch, Jack, "Jack Welch: 'Rank-and-Yank'? That's Not How It's Done," *The Wall Street Journal*, November 14, 2013.

5

Recruiting Job Candidates

Case 5.1. The Recruiting Process: The Growth of E-Recruitment in Recruiting Job Candidates

The most popular place to look for prospective employees used to be classified ads in newspapers. However, electronic recruitment (e-recruitment) in the last few years has certainly taken the number one spot for finding new employees.

What are the different type of e-recruitment platforms? They include websites such as Facebook, Blogs, Google+, LinkedIn, Myspace, Podcasts, Twitter, YouTube, and Monster.com. Each form of e-recruitment is a growing area for human resources to find prospective employees.

Companies used to be able to communicate in a downward, one-way fashion when the only real form of looking for prospective employees were newspaper advertisements. Social media sites such as Facebook, Twitter, and LinkedIn create a more two-way shared communication process. For example, one human resource manager likes to review the LinkedIn account of upcoming interviewees. She likes to have a general idea of what the interviewee looks like to help greet the person when he or she arrives at the reception desk at her company. Employers and prospective employees can engage in a dialogue by interacting online about the specific job opening. Even simple e-mail exchanges, arranging the date and time for the interview, can create a bond between the interviewer and the candidate.

Using social media as a recruitment tool does require considering many issues that didn't quite exist before the widespread use of the Internet. For example, a positive use of social media would be a prospect who posts well-written responses using Twitter or Facebook. Such people might show knowledge or an understanding of the industry for which they are applying. For example, an applicant might demonstrate the knowledge to be a sports information director if he or she demonstrates good writing skills and an understanding of college athletics. A candidate who discusses Adobe Photoshop skills and experiences would be a potentially good fit for graphic design positions.

However, just as with face-to-face interviews, the HR person wants to be careful about the legal issues of conducting a search online. Monster.com suggests that HR people use social media after the first live interview so they don't make a quick judgment based on what they see online. Plus, reviewing social media should be conducted at the same time in the search process for each candidate to be fair in the evaluation process.[1]

Unlike other platforms, such as Twitter or Facebook, LinkedIn focuses on the business environment. LinkedIn has over 364 million members in 200 countries and territories. There are over 39 million students on LinkedIn. People who go to LinkedIn are interested in finding people they have worked with or would like to meet in regard to their career. Each user maintains an account and approves connections with other people. A user can ask to form a connection or, likewise, be asked to join someone else's connection. The list of connections can be used as a contact list, to follow specific companies, or to look for jobs, people, and business ideas.[2]

LinkedIn allows companies to create a job posting with a job description, experience required, and educational requirements. Employers can also reach out to specific users to gauge their interest in a job opening. At the same time, individuals can choose to contact the employer to help show their interest.

When creating a professional network online, the first step is for users to include a picture that reflects that you are professional in your field. You want to portray yourself as being a professional. Having an interesting but professional picture can attract the attention of potential employers. For example, if you were looking for a writing position, you might wear a large brim fedora hat to show you possess some creative ideas that could be used in public relations and advertising positions.

Many companies have denied giving a job candidate a position because either they or their friends have posted embarrassing photos or used improper language. A recent college senior wasn't offered a job at an accounting firm because of a picture posted by a friend on Facebook. Although the picture was only of the two friends sharing a selfie and a drink, the accounting firm felt the applicant would not be a proper fit.

A second piece of advice is to keep your status area updated with current work, education, and experiences. Third, complete all pages about yourself to help prospective employers learn about you quickly. And fourth, don't just focus on your latest job. The employer might like something you did in a previous job or charity where you donated time.[3] One recent applicant traveled throughout Europe right after college graduation. Upon returning home, he was interviewed by two large insurance companies. The insurance company recruiters were interested in him because he showed the ability to travel overseas. The recruiters felt the ability to travel globally would be a valuable skill for their insurance companies since they had operations in different countries.

Case Questions

1. Why is a newspaper classified as a one-communication vehicle compared to a two-way process, such as Twitter or LinkedIn?

2. Why would the human resources department of a company not like to use Twitter, Facebook, or LinkedIn?

3. Why would human resources like to use Twitter, Facebook, or LinkedIn?

4. Should college students have a Facebook, Twitter, or LinkedIn account?

5. Review your own Facebook, Twitter, or LinkedIn account and indicate which of them should be modified before going on an interview.

Case 5.2. Internal Versus External Candidates: Which Candidate Is More Valuable?

Organizational Recruiting Considerations

Organizations need to build a list of internal employees who can be tapped when high-level employees change companies, retire, or pass away. Much like a baseball team, there must be good people on the bench in lower-level positions ready to take the place of players/employees who are no longer able to do their job.

Internal recruiting involves filling job openings with current employees or people the employees know. Promotion from within means the organization posts job openings on company-wide e-mail, company newsletters, bulletin boards, and other internal mechanisms to promote the open positions. Employee referrals are a second type of internal recruiting. Referrals mean employees are encouraged to refer friends and relatives to apply for a position.

The advantage of internal recruiting is that it increases employee commitment and job satisfaction because employees feel they have an opportunity to advance in the company; the employee already works for the company, which shows interest in working at the company; the company already has knowledge of the employee's work habits; and it is often quicker and less costly than a full external search.

The disadvantage of searching to fill positions internally in the company is the pool of potential applicants is much smaller; there may be better qualified applicants in the external pool of prospects; employees will feel that they are guaranteed to fill open positions, which will lead to a lack of new people who can provide new ideas and creativity; and success in a lower-level position does not mean the employee will be successful in the higher-level position.

External recruitment also has advantages and disadvantages when a company is looking to fill a position. External recruiting sources include people who walk in to the position either in-person or online, recruitment at high schools and colleges, employment agencies that focus on finding talented employees to match with job openings, and advertisements online, in newspapers, and through various media.

External recruitment will lead to new people being hired who should have innovative ideas to operate the company. We can also find people who have experience in the position we are trying to fill. However, new people might cause some disruption in the way things are normally done, which can cause some conflict. External recruitments can take more time and will cost more money than an internal search. Most important, the internal candidate might have a nice looking résumé and references, but the company has no real data to support the assumption the employee is a good fit for the open position.

Amanda Clark is an internal candidate for an open assistant director position at the nonprofit community center where she has worked for nearly 30 years. Amanda has a bachelor's degree in education and was a program director for teens for 9 months of the year. She would then switch hats and become the summer camp director for the remaining three months. She ran the youth theater group for the nonprofit community center. She was also involved in finding 50 teenagers to participate in a summer sport tournament. The list of tasks she completed is extensive and would be hard to list in its entirety.

However, Amanda had two male direct superiors. She always got along well with the director, Bob Gold, and the assistant director, Mike Woods. Bob decided to retire, and Mike was appointed to be the new director of the Community Center. Mike was an internal candidate who had spent 25 years preparing to succeed Bob as director.

An external recruitment search began to find a new assistant director. This is where the case becomes interesting. The nonprofit placed an advertisement to the public in various local and national newspapers and websites looking for talented external candidates. But Mike never looked for internal candidates, such as Amanda, to be promoted to the assistant director position.

An external candidate, Sam Riddle, was hired after a lengthy 9-month search to fill the position. Sam worked in a management position at a hardware store 1,500 miles away. He created a hostile work environment, where at least half of the employees did not appreciate his in-your-face management style.

At the same time, Amanda was sought out by a local for-profit competitor to run its new youth facility. She would be in charge of the daycare facility and summer camp. Feeling overlooked at the nonprofit community center, she was honored to be asked to work at the local competitor only five minutes away. She accepted the job at the new for-profit organization. As an external candidate, Amanda was sure she was selected to use her experience and creativity to help build the for-profit youth facility.

At the nonprofit community center, Sam Riddle lasted about 3 years in his role as assistant director. He apparently interviews very well, since he was promoted to be a director at another facility within the organization.

Amanda used her great enthusiasm to build the daycare and camp at the new for-profit company. She left after about a year due to the lack of ethics on the part of management. The for-profit was a family-owned business that was generally well operated. However, there was one family member who helped manage Amanda's facility who was hard to manage and would routinely make mistakes, such as leaving children unattended.

Amanda was fortunate to return to her original nonprofit organization and to work part-time helping the programs that are most dear to her heart. She was paid an hourly wage, instead of her previous full-time pay. She applied for the now vacant job of assistant director. At this point, Amanda is unsure if she is considered an internal or external candidate at the nonprofit community center.

Case Questions

1. Did the original nonprofit appear to develop internal candidates?

2. If the agency didn't develop internal candidates, why do you think this would happen?

3. Did the nonprofit develop and use its bench strength?

4. At what point(s) was Amanda an external candidate?

5. Is it better to hire from within or outside your organization?

Notes

1. Berkowitz, Melanie, "Social Media Recruiting: Understand the Legal Guidelines," *Monster. com*, retrieved September 19, 2015.
2. Archanal, L, V. G. Nivya, and S. M. Thankam, "Recruitment Through Social Media Area: Human Resource," *ISOR Journal of Business and Management*, 2014, pp. 37–41.
3. Kane, Libby, "8 Mistakes You Should Never Make on LinkedIn," *Forbes.com*, March 4, 2013.

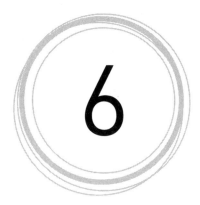

6

Selecting New Employees

Case 6.1. The Selection Process:
Searching for a New Faculty Member . . .
What Step in the Selection Process Are We in Today?

There are many potential steps in the selection process to complete when conducting a search process to fill an open position. Most important, companies need to follow the Uniform Guidelines on Employee Selection Process (UGESP) to avoid discriminatory hiring practices. The guidelines were designed to ensure that organizations were using nondiscriminatory employment practices so they would be in compliance under the Civil Rights Act of 1964, often referred to as Title VII.[1]

The following steps are part of a typical employee selection process:

1. Application and/or résumé collection and review.

2. Preliminary screening. May include a quick look into background check.

3. Organize initial interview with promising candidates.

4. Complete written and physical tests if necessary.

5. Secondary interviews for candidates who passed the first interview.

6. Detailed background check of references, criminal history, drug screening, and web searches if appropriate to the position.

7. Position offered to selected candidate. If position is accepted, prospect is hired and process is ended. If position is declined, search committee decides whether to offer position to second highest rated candidate.

Small-Time College is looking for a good accountant that has the right personality-job fit to complement its existing accounting faculty. Accounting positions often require the accountant to work closely with financial statements, such as income statements and balance sheets. However, Small-Time College also wants to hire a professor who likes to build close relationships with students and help them be involved in donating time to nonprofit organizations. The college intends to hire a CPA to be sure there is a good ability-job fit and hopes the new professor will have a good person-organization fit, which means the new professor will fit into the culture of the entire company.

The following are some of the selection steps taken at Small-Time College in its search for a new full-time accounting professor.

1. A search committee is formed to search for the new accounting professor. Professors from the Division of Business and a professor from outside the division are included on the committee.

2. Search committee works together to write a job description and an advertisement for the open accounting position.

3. HR places the advertisement in various media, such as Monster.com and Higherjobs.com. The advertisement's job was tailored to find qualified applicants who could teach upper-level accounting courses on-campus and off-campus, online and face-to-face, while also participating in college-wide activities.

ASSISTANT PROFESSOR OF ACCOUNTING

Apply for Position

Institution: Small-Time College

Location: Carlsbad, CA

Category: Faculty—Business/Accounting

Posted: 06/18/2016

Application Due: Open Until Filled

Type: Full Time

Assistant Professor of Accounting

The Division of Business at Small-Time College located in Carlsbad, CA, invites applications for the position of full-time, tenure track Assistant Professor of Accounting Faculty position reporting to the Chair of the Division of Business.

This faculty position is primarily responsible for traditional and online course development and instruction in the Accounting Bachelor of Arts Degree at the traditional based campus programs, the online and F2F undergraduate off-campus degree completion programs, and the Accounting track in the MBA program. Courses can include, but are not limited to, Accounting Information Systems, Advanced Cost Accounting, Auditing, and Financial Management. Potential graduate-level courses include Corporate Tax and Nonprofit and Government Accounting.

The faculty member is also responsible for actively participating in all aspects of college community (teaching, scholarship, and service) in alignment with the faculty handbook and to serve a primary role in the governance and organization of the program, including academic planning, curriculum development and review, advising and program improvement.

Duties and Responsibilities

- Assumes responsibility for assigned course instruction online, off-campus, and on-campus in both undergraduate and graduate courses.
- Facilitates learning and caring environment, which encourages critical thinking, investigation, self-direction, and respect for the uniqueness of each individual.
- Leads and/or participates in course development, curriculum planning, implementation, and evaluation.
- Completes required CPE and maintains current license.
- Attends Business Club meetings with senior accounting students.
- Assists students in finding internships at local area CPA and other firms.
- Coordinates students to perform internship and community service at the Volunteer Income Tax Assistance (VITA).
- Supports the collection of IACBE results related to the accounting students on campus and off-campus.
- Demonstrates knowledge of and implementation of the general education philosophy.
- Serves on College committees as appointed or elected.
- Participates in peer, self, and course review.
- Promotes the mission and purposes of the College in various internal and external activities.
- Evaluates student progress and maintains appropriate records.
- Advises students in course-related matters and makes referrals to appropriate resources.
- Remains current with the trends, issues, and practices in the discipline.
- Actively involved in professional development and scholarly activities.
- Assists the Chair of the department with administrative tasks as needed and appointed.
- Participates in recruitment and retention efforts, specific to the program, as needed.
- Performs other duties as assigned.
- Contributes to the evaluation of student academic achievement and other evaluative processes of the College.
- Adheres to College and System policies and procedures as indicated in the Faculty Handbook, College policies, and in other applicable regulatory documents.
- Upholds, promotes, and demonstrates behaviors consistent with the Mission and Core Values (Faith, Community, Justice, and Excellence) of the College.

Minimum Qualifications

CPA or CMA (current license) with a Master's degree in the accounting field. Must have significant experience in the field of accounting, possess effective oral and written communication and interpersonal skills, documented excellence in online teaching,

(Continued)

(Continued)

and be committed to the concepts of innovation and excellence in accounting education. Candidate must maintain active and current membership in professional and community organizations. The candidate must effectively use Microsoft Office Suite software and other accounting software.

Preferred Qualifications

Doctorate degree (related field). College-level teaching experience in accounting and experience with web-based course delivery and instructional technology are highly desirable. Learning Management System experience preferred, Moodle experience highly preferred. Ability to use Sage 50/QuickBooks and SAP software is very desirable.

To Apply

Send cover letter, transcripts, CV/résumé, a statement of teaching philosophy and contact information for three (3) professional references (as Word or PDF attachments) via email to: bannisterm@.edu or by regular mail to Dr. Maxwell Bannister, Chair of the Division of Business, Small-Time College, 291 Golf Ball Street, Carlsbad, CA 01050.
    Review of applications begins immediately and will continue until the position is filled.

4. Résumés (in education they are called CVs) are collected and distributed among the committee members.

5. Preliminary screening requires weeding out the applicants who don't meet the minimum qualifications. The process includes a meeting to drop those candidates who didn't have a CPA or a Master's in accounting. The next step could be to drop those candidates who lack teaching experience. There is a great deal of debate deciding on the top 10 candidates if you have a pile of about 100 applicants. The top 10 applicants are then called by the HR Department to see if they are still interested in the position and if they would be able to accept the position within the salary range the professor is expected to be paid. The salary range is determined by the salaries offered to similar faculty at Small-Time College.

6. Selection interviews: The top 10 candidates are often reduced to the top three to five candidates if they are still interested in the position and the salary range. The final five candidates are then called to arrange a date and time for their initial interview. Sometimes, all the candidates are interviewed on the same day. That makes a long day for the search committee and HR. Otherwise, it is important to interview candidates in as few days as possible.

7. Conducting the interview actually starts before the actual interviews. The committee often creates a list of appropriate questions that will be asked to all applicants. Each person on the committee often asks specific questions related to his or her personal area of expertise (which could be teaching accounting courses,

experience advising students, or working with students on projects outside the classroom). This ensures that all candidates are asked the same questions.

Once the interview begins, it is important to review the realistic job preview (RJP) and make sure the candidate understands the nature of the job. The RJP is a review of all of the tasks and requirements of the job, both good and bad. The committee will want to make sure the candidates have as much information as possible about the job so they are aware of the tasks to be completed if they are offered the position.

8. Background checks (which can include reference checks, credit checks, criminal background checks, and web checks) need to be used in a professional and ethical manner. For example, reference checks should not be conducted without the consent of the candidate. It is important to research only for relevant data. There is no need to dig for information beyond the scope of the search. Keep the search related to the specific information for the job that is being filled.[2]

    Reference checks often confirm a candidate did work at a previous organization. But it is important to understand that candidates don't pick references unless they are most likely going to give them a positive referral. Web searches on sites such as LinkedIn have become more popular as a source for checking the candidate's background and references.

9. Selecting the candidate and offering the job often means the top two candidates are asked to return for a second interview. They most likely will meet the dean and Small-Time College president. The final decision normally rests with the college president, who decides what is best for the college. Offering the job to the candidate is not quite as simple as it sounds. The candidate might decide to stay with his or her current employer or might disagree on salary, a certain benefit, or even the job itself. If the first candidate decides not to accept the position, the search committee, dean, and president have to decide if they would like to offer the job to the second candidate or do an entirely new search.

Case Questions

1. What would be a good personality fit for an accounting professor at Small-Time College?

2. Should the preliminary screening process result in a top 10 of applicants?

3. What is the role of the Uniform Guidelines on Employee Selection Process (UGESP)?

4. Which step did the case skip in regard to the steps in the selection process?

5. Why are background checks harder to conduct than it might appear?

Case 6.2. Looking for "Organizational Fit": Walter's Unstructured Interview at Google

Walter was proud to earn his bachelor's degree in computer science from Small-Time College in California. That was almost three years ago, and he felt as if it was even longer since the field of computer science changes so quickly.

Walter was able to find a nice "Comp Sci" job at Small-Time College. He interviewed for the job and remembers the key questions were what his greatest strengths (which he answered as programming skills) and his greatest weakness (he didn't have one prepared to discuss) were. Walter considered this a structured interview since one of the interviewers from Small-Time College said she was responsible for asking certain questions. After working for three years at Small-Time College, Walter felt he had a good personality-job fit, since he was a valuable member of the Information Technology Department. Walter also felt he had proven he had good ability-job fit, since his three years of experience as a computer programmer at the college proved he had the skills to complete the job. Most important, Walter felt he had a perfect person-organization fit, since he was liked by everyone at the college and fit in very well in the educational culture.

Recently, Walter was contacted by someone on LinkedIn to apply for a new position at Google. Like everyone else, Walter had heard stories that Google was a great place to work. He even watched the movie *The Intern* to get a better glimpse of what takes place at Google.

Walter also researched the company (using Google Search) and found out Google uses a unique way to find and match people with jobs at the amazing company.[3]

First, Google used its extremely creative way of thinking to create a vice-president of people operations. Like most companies, Walter's current employer calls this position the vice-president of human resources.

Second, Google uses its data analysis skills to analyze vast amounts of data about what works and what doesn't work during the hiring process. One result they found was that interviews had a zero relationship with the success the person actually had on the job. Consequently, Google doesn't believe in the traditional metrics used in the hiring process. These traditional metrics include GPA, SAT scores, or the prestige of college the candidate attended. Instead, creative companies like Google measure a candidate on behaviors, such as their level of happiness, ability to work well with other people, if they like a challenge, if they seek information, and if they are willing to adapt.[4]

Walter spoke to the assistant in people operations and set up an interview for one week later. He was warmly received by Google and quickly fell in love with the colorful and wide open layout of the headquarters. In a casual and relaxed atmosphere, he sat down with three different Google employees and basically explained how he grew up in California and what led him down the path of computer science.

Walter thought he might be asked one of those out-of-the-box interview questions, such as how many gasoline stations would you expect to find in a city of 160,000 people. But his research also uncovered that Google felt these types of questions were biased since they tended to just make the interviewer look smart since they had time to work out the answers.

Since Walter wanted to be a good match, he went with the flow of the interview and became much more relaxed than he could remember in his interview with his current company. He expressed how he liked being happy at work, enjoyed programming computers with a team of employees, and especially enjoyed interacting with clients to help them solve their problems. Walter enjoyed the unstructured interview and felt he was doing a good job interacting with the Google interviewers. He expected the Google interview was going to a least be a semi-structured interview, which would combine some preplanned and some unplanned questions. However, the Google interviewers appeared to not have any prepared questions and instead asked all unplanned questions.

Walter went on to explain how he had been promoted three times in three years and enjoyed the challenge each positioned offered. He liked the "go for it attitude" at his present employer. Walter also knew from his research that Google liked outgoing, happy employees that worked well with their fellow workers and customers.

In the end, Walter did not get the job for reasons he never learned. Although he was disappointed, he also knew that Facebook once turned down Brian Acton for a job and he went on to co-found WhatsApp which he sold to Facebook for $19 billion.[5] Walter hoped a similar fate was in his future and he could one day sell his ideas to Google.

Walter went back to his current job with renewed passion and energy. He was excited to have spent time at Google and hoped to bring back some of what he learned and apply it to his own job and division. He also intended to work closer than ever with his own Human Resources Department to look for opportunities in his current company. He was hoping to find a "fast track" program that would speed up his own development, so he could create a more open and creative company culture along the way.

Walter always wondered what his life would have been like if he had been hired by Google. He thought he was going to be an excellent fit in the Google organizational culture. He felt he had a good personality-job fit since he demonstrated in the interviews that he was an outgoing computer programmer who would work well with Google's unique corporate culture. Walter also felt he was a great candidate in regard to ability-job fit since his three years of experience in his current programming job showed he could apply his technical skills as a computer programmer in a work environment. Walter also felt he was a good person-organization fit since he would work very well within Google's creative-organizational culture. In the end, Walter was happy to grow from the experience of trying to get a job at Google. He definitely had more appreciation for his current job since his employer had been smart enough to give him a job three years before. He was ready to repay that by doing an excellent job going into the future.

Case Questions

1. What do you think the vice president of people actually does at Google?

2. Did Walter experience a structured, semistructured, or unstructured interview when he first left college?

3. What are your own greatest strengths and weaknesses as a prospective employee?

4. How would you answer if someone in HR asked you an unstructured question such as how many gas stations there are in a city of 160,000?

5. Design a form to help Google compare different candidates. HINT: You can list some different names of people in the rows. The column headings need to represent the areas where Google is looking for in an interview (Happy Employees, Employees Willing to Take on a Challenge, Creative Employees, etc.)

6. Why do you think Google felt Walter was not a good organizational fit for the company?

Notes

1. http://www.uniformguidelines.com/uniformguidelines.html.
2. Lu, Andrew, "5 Tips to Keep Reference Checks Legal," *FindLaw.com*, December 12, 2012.
3. Nisen, Max, "Moneyball at Work: They've Discovered What Really Makes a Great Employee at Work," *Business Insider*, May 6, 2013.
4. Nisen, Max, "Google HR Boss Explains Why GPA and Most Interviews Are Useless," *Business Insider*, June 19, 2013.
5. Wood, Zoe, "Facebook Turned Down WhatsApp Co-Founder Brian Acton for Job in 2009," *The Guardian*, February 20, 2014.

DEVELOPING AND MANAGING

PART III

7

Training, Learning, Talent Management, and Development

Case 7.1. The Need for Training and Development: Should You Use Massive Open Online Courses (MOOCs) Such as Coursera and Udacity to Recruit and Retain Talent?

Juan Salmeron graduated from Small-Town College two years ago and was excited to land a job in customer service with AT&T. He rose quickly in stature at the local AT&T office and became the go-to guy when someone needed to understand some new technology.

After 2 years, Juan figured he was marketable and wanted to see if he could land a larger position with another firm. He worked hard on his résumé, cover letter, references, and copies of his college transcripts.

Juan interviewed well at California Mutual Insurance (CMI), and his dreams came true! Juan was hired as a corporate trainer. His job responsibility was to teach the insurance employees at CMI about how to use the latest technology to improve their own performance on the job.

Thus, Juan had to develop a process to help teach the insurance employees about technology in the workplace. The obvious option was to actually hold courses at CMI's headquarters. Realistically, Juan could offer two or three courses a week. But each employee would have to leave desk and job duties to attend the face-to-face (F2F) training courses.

Juan could also try to hire experts in technology topics, and they could then develop a course to train the insurance employees. However, this would require extra financial costs to hire the expert and videotape the lectures. Juan could also decide to hold courses in a synchronous or asynchronous distance learning format. *Synchronous*

36

distance learning occurs when the trainer/teacher and his employees/pupils interact in different places, but during the same time. Thus, students and the trainer might select Tuesday night as the time when they hold the training class. The trainer could be on his or her laptop computer at home, and the employees could access their training course at night. On Tuesday night, there would be a specific class where the trainer and all the students would meet online and discuss the material to learn. Synchronous learning would require the trainer and employee to meet at a specific time.

Asynchronous distance learning occurs when the trainer and the employee interact at different times. Students enrolled in an asynchronous course are able to complete their work within a certain time period. Thus the employee would access the learning site within a time period such as one week. The employee would review the material, watch videos, and take any exams, as necessary. Thus, the trainer and employee would have more freedom to complete assignments within a pre-established time period.

As a third option, Juan could use massive open online courses (MOOCs) offered by online providers such as Coursera and Udacity. MOOCs are free online courses offered by experts at no cost. MOOC course topics range from law, education, engineering, management, and all areas of technology. As Coursera explains: "Coursera is an education platform that partners with top universities and organizations worldwide, to offer courses online for anyone to take, for free. Learners can choose from hundreds of courses created by the world's top educational institutions. Courses are open to anyone, and learning is free."[1]

For example, Juan could encourage his employees to take a course on Gamification. Gamification is a course offered at the University of Pennsylvania, through Coursera, and taught by Associate Professor Kevin Werbach from The Wharton School of Business. The initial section of the course had 80,000 students followed by a section of 63,000 students.[2]

Gamification is taught in four to eight weekly modules and is offered in different languages. *Gamification* is the adaptation of digital game technology applied to human resource and other business issues. Thus, Juan's employees could learn to develop a game, whereby their customers are rewarded points or in-game rewards for checking their insurance policies, investment accounts, and so forth on a regular basis. The goal is to make "the game" addictive so that customers check their own accounts on a more regular basis. The idea is to simulate games such as Angry Birds where customers actually want to check their accounts.

Many people in HR feel MOOCs could be a major part of recruiting, training, and developing employees with online degree certifications.[3] Udacity has a program that allows employers to review the student résumés. Over 350 large organizations, such as Facebook, have paid Udacity and Coursera to match them with high performing students.[4]

MOOCs can have thousands of students sign up for a course online. Students often earn a certificate for completing the course. HR departments can also develop their own certificate or reward for their employees that complete a MOOC. Companies such as AT&T are using Udacity's MOOCs to train their employees in new areas of science and technology. Starbucks offers employees free tuition to participate in Arizona State University's online courses.

HR departments are also interested in recruiting people who have completed MOOCs. They were originally interested in students that completed a science- or technology-related course. Tech-oriented companies such as Amazon, Facebook, and Google have paid Udacity and Coursera to match them with their top students.

Case Questions

1. Would Coursera or Udacity be a viable option for all human resource departments to train their employees?

2. Would HR be eliminating themselves from their own job if they use Coursera?

3. Would MOOCs be a good recruiting method for attracting top talent?

4. Should Juan use a synchronous or asynchronous training format if he decides to use a MOOC to train his employees?

5. What are two advantages and two disadvantages of gamification of the HR functions?

Case 7.2. Talent Management and Development: The Talented Harry Saunders's Career Development at the Big Buy Supermarket

Developing talented employees requires planning on the part of human resources. The career of Harry Saunders is a good example. Harry progressed in his career by using three options: formal education, experience, and employee assessment.

Harry's father worked in the marketing department at The Big Buy Supermarket chain in Florida. With a little help from his father, Harry was able to get a job as a bag-boy during high school. Harry enjoyed using the cash register since he liked numbers. Harry also displayed social skills since he liked talking to customers.

After high school, Harry went to college and tried different business majors until he concentrated on accounting. Harry knew he had knack for numbers, and accounting came easy to him. After graduating from college, Harry was offered quite a few positions to work for local and national accounting firms. At such a firm, he would go on the road and conduct audits of his clients' accounting books. He would travel quite a bit—but he would be well paid and eventually would become a certified public accountant (CPA).

However, the HR Department at The Big Buy had no desire to lose an employee it felt had the potential to be a top-level manager. Thus, HR offered him a position in the accounting department at a competitive salary with the CPA firms. Since Harry liked working at The Big Buy, and even followed in his father's footsteps, he accepted the position.

Harry enjoyed organizing the accounting department at The Big Buy for nearly a decade. The supermarket chain grew to more than 100 stores. Harry felt he needed to get a graduate degree in marketing to help further his rise in management. The Big Buy offered 100 percent tuition reimbursement. It took Harry 2 years to complete his MBA in marketing.

After 20 years in accounting, Harry felt he was tired of running the same old accounting data. He was not as marketable as he once was because he had never become a CPA. He also missed working directly with customers.

Thus, Harry contacted HR, and they worked closely with him to find a new spot in the organization. Harry took a *psychological test,* which is a series of multiple choice questions about what motivated Harry in a work environment. The test results indicated Harry was equally happy working with data and people.

Harry was promoted to the new position of database marketing manager. In that position, Harry would work with large amounts of sales data that were being generated by the computer systems at the 100-plus stores Big Buy owned. Harry's job would be to analyze sales data to find products that were selling unusually well or poorly at each of the stores. Harry hired two young computer science majors to run the computer programs, sort the data, and help Harry make a weekly presentation to senior management about the results of the data.

Harry felt a strong resurgence in his career. He was thrilled to be working with customers again. He often visited stores to ask customers about various food items. He felt this boots-on-the-ground strategy would help him to better understand the overall sales data produced by his two employees back in the home office.

Harry became a popular speaker at supermarket conferences, as mining the data from large computer systems was an increasingly important task for all supermarket chains. Harry used his mathematical skills honed by a decade in accounting to understand the trends in food shopping. Harry was the first person to create a grocery store customer loyalty card, where shoppers paid $20 a year for the right to get lower prices on selected products. The idea of shoppers paying for a membership to buy groceries at a traditional supermarket was unheard of at the time Harry tested the idea. The result was that the customers of The Big Buy loved paying for the card so they would get lower prices on selected items throughout the store. Harry and his team could better track customer purchases and buying habits because shoppers were using their Big Buy card.

Harry took a few quiet moments to review his career by using the four stages of career development: Exploration, Establishment, Maintenance, and Disengagement. He felt fortunate to have started his career in the exploration stage by considering different job opportunities after he finished college. He experienced the establishment stage in his career by working in the accounting department for what felt like a long time—20 years. He feels refreshed to have transferred to marketing and has found the whole process of tracking customers a great part of the maintenance stage in his continued career at The Big Buy. Harry also felt he was in no rush to disengage from the company anytime in the near future. With the full support of his wife, Harry plans on working at The Big Buy instead of taking any type of early retirement offer.

Case Questions

1. How did Harry and HR use formal education to further his career?

2. How did employee assessment help Harry to advance?

3. Explain how Harry went through the career stages of Exploration, Establishment, Maintenance, and Disengagement.

4. What are some of the individual and organizational consequences that occurred as a result of the organizational career planning process at Big Buy?

5. Why did Harry's attitude and performance dramatically change after changing from the accounting to the marketing department?

Notes

1. https://www.coursera.org/about/.

2. McWilliams, Julie, "Coursera at Penn Surpasses One Million Enrollees," *Penn Current*, May 9, 2013.

3. Quinn, Jody, "Mining the MOOC: HR Looks to Online to Recruit and Train Employees," *Skilled Up.com*, August 25, 2014.

4. Wheeler, Kevin, "Why MOOC's Might Change Your Recruiting Methods," *ERE Media,* March 4, 2014.

8

Performance Management and Appraisal

Case 8.1. Why Do We Conduct Performance Appraisals? Jennee LeBeau and the Case of the Missing Performance Appraisal System

Jennee LeBeau was very excited to be hired as the director of human resources at Sunshine Hotels. Her office was located at the Main Island Hotel. Jennee spent her first year at Sunshine Hotels getting used to the processes used by HR. She spent most of her time in her office at Main Island Hotels. She didn't get to visit the other two Sunshine Hotels very often. Jennee's employees in HR like her hands-off supervisory style. However, they also feel she would be an even better supervisor if she left her office and interacted with the employees more often.

Jennee had spent the last 7 years as the assistant director of human resources for a chain of 10 fast-food restaurants. She figured being in charge of HR for a growing chain of three hotels would be similar to her experiences working in the fast-food industry.

While working in her office, she noticed Sunshine Hotels didn't conduct performance appraisals. Jennee thought performance appraisals (PA) were a common process in all companies. She was quite shocked at finding such a review process was not in place at Sunshine Hotels since they have nearly 30 employees. She decided the hotel chain was not overly concerned with evaluating employees in their first two hotels since the employees were mostly family and friends. But the addition of a third hotel has forced the Sunshine Hotel owners to create more HR policies, rules, and forms to make sure they are following all the laws of HR.

Jennee did some research and found that a performance appraisal is an ongoing process of evaluating employee performance. However, it is also a tool of the large process of having a *performance management system*, which is the process of identifying, measuring, managing, and developing the performance of the human resources in an organization. Thus, a PA is really a mechanism to help evaluate employees so they can develop into larger roles and to ensure the success of the company going into the future.

The good news is that Jennee figured out she could start from scratch and develop her own performance management system (PMS). She figured she could set up an entirely new PMS. PAs of individuals could be part of an ongoing process of evaluating employees.

Jennee has to decide what will be included in her new PMS. She wants the PA to collect *valid information*. That means what she measures must be true and correct. She wants to be sure to measure the performance process. Although Jennee wants to collect valid information, she also has to be concerned that the process isn't overly long or costly. She figures she can keep costs lower by emailing the PA to each employee to reduce mailing costs. She also wanted to use a multiple choice style PA so she could easily quantify the results.

The PA also has to be reliable. She has to trust that the performance data collected are consistent and that the PA works the same each time she uses it.

Jennee wants the employees to accept the process as important to their own career development. *Acceptability* means that the use of PA is satisfactory or appropriate to the employees that will use the PA to improve their work performance.

Jennee also wants to develop a process that would not be overly expensive or time consuming to implement. If the PA is overly long to complete, then the manager and employee will not use the PA as a tool to improve performance.

The PA has to be specific about an employee's job performance so that it is a useful instrument for improving areas that need development for that specific employee.

Another important goal is the PA has to help achieve the mission and goals of Sunshine Hotels. Completing the PA process should help employees better understand what Sunshine expects from them and how they can complete their own job to help the company fulfill its mission.

Jennee is starting to realize that she has walked into a very large project in designing a PMS from scratch. She is starting to realize she will need to organize a committee to help develop the process, especially the PA form. In answering her own questions, she realized she will be putting together a PA that Sunshine employees will be using for the first time. Employees currently receive a straight raise across the board. If the owners of Sunshine Hotels determine everyone deserves a 3 percent raise, then all employees get the raise irrespective of their own work performance. A new performance management system and performance appraisal process will most likely make it easier to administer raises based on the rating each employee receives as part of the process. However, the employees might prefer the across-the-board raises rather than having to personally earn their raises.

Jennee decided to create a first draft of her performance appraisal form. She can show this draft to her committee. The following is Jennee's performance appraisal:

PERFORMANCE APPRAISAL FORM

NAME: _____

HOTEL: _____

DEPARTMENT and JOB TITLE: _____

DATE OF APPRAISAL: _____

FROM: _____ TO: _____

Employee Signature _____

Employer Signature _____

	Exceptional	Successful	Needs Improvement	Unsatisfactory
Demonstrates Required Job Knowledge				
Quality of Work & Productivity				
Makes Effective Decisions				
Builds and Maintains Relationships With Others				
Communicates Effectively				
Exhibits Supervisory Abilities				
Overall Performance Appraisal Plan of Action				

Case Questions

1. What is the real goal(s) of a performance appraisal?

2. How can Jennee be sure to collect valid and reliable data with her new performance system?

3. How can Jennee get the employees to accept the process as important to their own career development?

4. Can Jennee develop a process that is not overly expensive to conduct with employees?

5. Complete the performance appraisal form in the case using Jennee LeBeau as the employee you are rating. Assume you are Patrick Staal, who is the chief financial officer (CFO) who is rating Jennee's first year of performance.

EMPLOYEE PERFORMANCE APPRAISAL FORM

NAME: Jennee LeBeau
HOTEL: Main Island
DEPARTMENT & JOB TITLE: Director of Human Resources
DATE OF APPRAISAL:
FROM: January 1, 2016 TO: December 31, 2016
Employee Signature: Jennee LeBeau
Supervisor Signature: Patrick Staal

	Exceptional	Successful	Needs Improvement	Unsatisfactory
Demonstrates Required Job Knowledge	X			
Quality of Work & Productivity	X			
Makes Effective Decisions	X			
Builds & Maintains Relationships With Others			X	

	Exceptional	Successful	Needs Improvement	Unsatisfactory
Communicates Effectively			X	
Exhibits Supervisory Abilities			X	
Overall Performance Appraisal Plan of Action	Jennee LeBeau has been the Director of Human Resources for the last year. She has excellent knowledge of the human resource concerns at Main Island Hotel.	As the Director of HR. Jennee is well liked. However, there is room for improvement since she spends most of the time in her office.	Jennee needs to develop better social skills. Developing better social skills will help her to improve her communication and supervisory abilities.	Jennee will participate in team building sessions to improve her communication and supervisory skills.

Case 8.2. Performance Appraisal Problems: The Trouble With Performance Systems

It is unfortunate that employees fear their performance appraisal since the goal of a performance management system is to help employees develop. However, sitting across a table from your manager and discussing your performance record is most likely going to be a high-stress situation.

Janice Flahive didn't look forward to her performance appraisal. As an advertising salesperson for her local newspaper, the *Miami News*, it was Janice's job to sell advertising space in the newspaper. Her performance was mainly based upon how much ad space she sold. Janice felt she should have also been evaluated on customer satisfaction, creating new accounts, or developing relationships with prospective businesses that could lead to future sales opportunities. Instead, Janice's performance appraisals usually ended up being a one-way communication process where her employer criticized her for not selling enough advertising space.

The PMS process is full of potential problems if it is not administered properly. Many of these problems occur because managers are not properly trained to administer a performance management system. The lack of training can lead to "rating errors," where one manager grades employees easier than a fellow manager who is a tougher grader. The result of inconsistent grading can lead to star employees receiving the same grades as weaker employees.

Poorly trained managers do not provide continuous feedback to their employees. Feedback is provided only during the performance appraisal meeting. Managers need to provide performance feedback more often and document their interactions with the employee. It cannot be stressed enough that managers need to document, document, and collect even more documentation on each employee under their supervision. Documentation is needed to support strong employees for raises and promotions. Even more important, documentation is critical if an employee needs to be reprimanded or fired as a result of the performance appraisal.

Much in the manner of Janice's experience, performance appraisals often fail to critique the employee in all areas of performance. Janice's job is in sales, which makes it easier to evaluate her in that area since sales can be quantified—she either makes her sales quota or she doesn't. However, Janice still deserves to be evaluated on qualitative areas such as customer service skills or leadership ability, which are often not able to be quantified.

Janice's performance appraisals should help her to develop into a better salesperson and potential management leader. It appears that Janice's performance appraisal is a meeting that tends to discuss her past performance. Instead, the meeting should help Janice to develop a performance plan with specific goals for the coming year.

One of the more controversial rating systems is the ranking method. Ranking is a performance appraisal method that is used to evaluate employees from best to worst. At the *Miami News*, Janice's office is evaluated using the ranking system. Since the rank order is posted in the office, Janice knows she is currently seventh on the list of 10 employees. The list is as follows as it is displayed outside the human resources office:

1. Samuel Garcia

2. Rosa McGowan

3. Meghan Shotland

4. Albert Smithfield

5. Jerry Jones

6. Samantha Barron

7. Janice Flahive

8. Karreem Rush

9. Monique Wayne

10. Sarah Badlementi

Janice is concerned that her company will decide to keep the top three star employees, try to develop the next three employees, and try to lay off the bottom four employees.

Although there are many potential problems with a PMS that is not well organized, such a system is still very much needed in all organizations. Dr. Samuel Culbert, professor of management from UCLA, does not believe in the performance review; he supports a *performance preview*. This would be where Janice and her manager would sit down and together discuss how they can each help improve her overall performance. Janice can write "I" statements such as, "I will increase the amount of time I spend actually selling my products." Or, her employer might say, "I will check in with Janice on a monthly basis, instead of every six months."[1]

Another option for improving the performance appraisal system is to develop a team of people to review the employee. The traditional method is for the direct supervisor to evaluate his or her own employee. However, a more comprehensive 360-degree evaluation will analyze individual performance from many sides—from the supervisor's viewpoint, from subordinates' viewpoints, from the customers' viewpoints, from peers' viewpoints, and from a self-evaluation. Unfortunately, it will take extra time and money to collect data from all the different people who would be involved in that type of evaluation. However, the 360-degree evaluation might be worth the time and effort to help the employee develop under the guidance of multiple stakeholders instead of just the supervisor's.

Case Questions

1. Why are there problems with most performance management systems?

2. What is the potential problem with a performance review conducted by a team of managers?

3. Why is an "I" statement a good method for developing a positive PA?

4. What are the positive and negative aspects of using a ranking method at Janice's office at the *Miami News*?

5. What type of PA do you or did you have in the company you work or worked for?

Note

1. Culbert, Samuel A., "Get Rid of the Performance Review! It Destroys Morale, Kills Teamwork and Hurts the Bottom Line. And That's Just for Starters," *Wall Street Journal*, October 20, 2008.

Rights and Employee Management

Case 9.1. Coaching, Counseling, and Discipline: HR's Role—Document, Document, Document

Andrea Watson works in the small human resources department at ABC Fitness Center. There are currently about 50 employees working at ABC Fitness. Andrea enjoys the process of hiring and providing an orientation program for new employees. However, she does not like the responsibility of firing employees when they do not fit into the culture at ABC Fitness.

To overcome her own hesitation with firing employees, Andrea reviewed the *coaching* process, *counseling* process, *progressive discipline* process, and the *tests for just cause* used in disciplinary investigations. Andrea started to study and implement these processes about 2 years ago at ABC Fitness.

ABC Fitness uses the coaching process to give employees feedback to improve their performance over time. *Coaching* involves four steps: (1) describing the current performance, or what is currently being done by the employee; (2) describing the desired performance, or what the manager wants the employee to change; (3) getting a verbal commitment from the employee to change; and (4) following up to make sure the employee is behaving in the desired manner. Coaching is often associated with sports coaches such as Mike Krzyzewski at Duke University or Bill Belichick with the New England Patriots. However, coaching can be just as effective in a business situation as in sports. Employees in every organization need to receive positive feedback and support while doing their jobs.

Counseling is provided for employees who are not currently working at an acceptable level. Guidance is provided to help get the employee back on track. *Management counseling* involves giving the employee feedback so he or she knows a problem is affecting job performance. Employees with severe personal problems can be referred for help to the employee assistance program (EAP) to get assistance.

Unfortunately, some employees just cannot get their work performance to an acceptable level. Progressive discipline is then used to try to solve minor disciplinary infractions. *Progressive discipline* is a series of steps to help provide discipline:

Step 1. Informal talk

Step 2. Oral warning

Step 3. Written warning

Step 4. Suspensions

Step 5. In some cases, demotion or transfer, or

Step 6. Dismissal

A key element in disciplinary investigations is *just cause*. Just cause is a set of standards used to test for fairness in an organizational setting to ensure that any disciplinary action taken has reasonable cause. The tests attempt to ensure that the individual knew what the rules were, that there was reasonable evidence or proof that the person violated or disobeyed the rules, and that, if the rules were violated, the disciplinary action was appropriate and fair.

Andrea wasn't sure if all of these processes were conducted in the case of Derek Struble. Derek was an employee who worked at ABC Fitness for the last 20 years. He didn't exhibit the greatest level of enthusiasm with the health center's fitness members, but he was also never rude. He assisted fitness members whenever they needed help.

Andrea reviewed Derek's file and found he was in a graduate, nonprofit management program, which was supported by ABC Fitness since it paid half the tuition. His file contained limited documentation that Derek was at times not as "cheery" or "happy" as one might expect at a fitness center. The file mentioned that Derek didn't generate enough personal fitness training, which members paid for and which helped finance the fitness center.

Andrea was fairly sure Derek wasn't fired due to gross negligence (such as leaving the fitness members unattended). Nor was he fired due to serious misconduct, such as hurting another employee or doing harm to the company. Actually, Derek was very actively trying to recruit new members to the facility.

Thus, Andrea wished she had more documentation that would show that Derek had been coached, counseled, or had even gone through progressive discipline. She could find in the file only some notes that Derek could be more pleasant and should improve the number of paid training sessions he conducted in the fitness center.

Andrea was also concerned with the fact that Derek was 39 years old. The Age Discrimination in Employment Act of 1967 prohibits discrimination against persons 40 years of age or older. Congress found that older workers were disadvantaged in their efforts to retain employment and especially in regaining employment when released from a job.[1] Since Derek was 39, he was certainly very close to age 40 and could file a lawsuit against the fitness center.

Andrea had a meeting scheduled with Derek later in the afternoon. Her major thought was something her former director of human resources at her last job used to say, "Document, document, document."

Case Questions

1. Do you believe Derek received any of the four steps in the coaching process?

2. Did Derek receive progressive discipline?

3. Was there just cause to discharge Derek?

4. Would you, from what you know, discharge Derek?

5. How would the Age Discrimination in Employment Act of 1967 apply if Derek was 40 years old?

Case 9.2. Trends and Issues in HRM: Mindfulness—a Thoughtful Theory About Leadership

Astrubal Gonzalez worked as the food service manager at Big-Time Hospital in New Haven, Connecticut. Unfortunately, the food at the hospital was viewed as terrible. Still, since Astrubal's food service was the only place in the hospital to get food, sales were stable.

The CEO of the hospital, Jean Curry, wondered how she could improve the quality of the food in Big-Time Hospital. Her first priority was to create a change process to help the food service employees who were in denial that their food quality could be improved. She had to help them forget about the daily grind they had repeated for years and learn a new way to do their jobs. She had to get past their resistance to change and help them see that a modern food service operation could lift employee morale around the hospital.

On the way to work on the train, Jean happened to read about an interesting leadership theory called *mindfulness*. She thought mindfulness sounded like a process with which the employees could develop a renewed sense of mission toward delivering better food quality and service. She decided to contact human resources about exploring mindfulness as a way to replace mindlessness.

The human resources department responded by researching mindfulness as soon as it received the call from the CEO. If Jean Curry called, HR was certainly going to respond. The first step required defining leadership and mindfulness.

Leadership is the process of influencing employees to work toward the achievement of organizational objectives. In Jean's case, she was the leader, and it was her idea that using mindfulness might be the solution to motivating her food service personnel.

HR found out that mindfulness is an area of leadership study that has become more popular in the last decade. There are numerous summits and conferences devoted to teaching the process of mindfulness. Jon Kabat-Zinn, former professor at the University of Massachusetts Medical School, describes mindfulness as "paying attention in a particular way: on purpose, in the present moment and non-judgmentally."[2]

By comparison, mindlessness refers to our subconscious, out-of-habit, or repetitious actions, placing limitations on what we can accomplish. A mindless worker would rather continue the same steps and procedures used in the past at work.

Mindfulness enables employees to be fully aware of their mind, body, and spirit. Mindful people are fully aware of what is happening around them. A mindful employee has a high level of self-confidence, which gives the employee the belief that failures and challenges can be overcome. Mindful people can visualize great change instead of placing limitations on what they can do to lead the organization.[3]

A mindful manager can lead the employees to reach higher levels of success. But to do this, the mindful manager needs to learn to be compassionate, more self-confident, and an authentic leader. Recent organizations to embrace mindfulness include Google, Harvard Business Schools, and the Seattle Seahawks football team in the NFL.[4]

Employees would most likely find it easier to enjoy mindlessness on a regular day at work. However, an organization needs to strive for mindfulness every day at work to help develop a company culture of innovation and creativity. Mindful employees look for new ways to solve problems. To help develop mindful employees, HR needs to set the standard by offering training on leadership concepts such as the benefits of mindfulness. HR and managers in the different divisions can work together to model the behavior of being mindful so that employees can learn to bounce back from failure, learn to be more confident, and thus be actively aware of their surroundings at work and in their industry.

Jean decided she was going to also have to learn to use mindfulness if she expected to have such a culture exist at her hospital. She had to exhibit behaviors that showed she was innovative and creative. She wanted to be a leader who embraced everything at work and shared the success with her employees.

After a series of training sessions led by HR, the food service personnel started to feel more self-confident about their jobs. They were encouraged and wanted to cook more creative lunch and dinner options. They were excited to see which new food options were well received by the employees of the hospital. When a food item was not well received, they didn't get disappointed as they would have in the past. They just used that experience as a learning situation. Their self-confidence and creativity were evident in the variety of food they offered and the upbeat customer service provided to their customers.

Jean was so excited about the results of implementing mindfulness that she was ready to spread the leadership theory throughout the entire Big-Time Hospital organization.

Case Questions

1. How does mindfulness compare to situational leadership?

2. How does mindfulness compare to the definition of leadership?

3. What are some ideas about how human resources can teach employees to be more mindful?

4. Do you think Astrubal will find it easy or difficult to become a mindful leader?

5. After mindful training, what could Astrubal do to show he is a more mindful manager?

6. How did Jean use the stages of the change process?

Notes

1. http://www.eeoc.gov/laws/statutes/adea.cfm.
2. Garms, Erica, "Practicing Mindful Leadership," *Association for Talent Development*, March 8, 2013, https://www.td.org/Publications/Magazines/TD/TD-Archive/2013/03/Practicing-Mindful-Leadership.
3. Moua, Mia, "Mindfulness and Self-Efficacy," *Leading With Cultural Intelligence*, http://catalog.flatworldknowledge.com/bookhub/reader/5575?e=moua_1.0-ch04#moua_1.0-ch05_s04.
4. http://www.mindfulleader.org/#home.

10

Employee and Labor Relations

Case 10.1. Unions and Labor Rights: Can Labor Unions and Management Work Together?

Candice works in the human resources department for Familia Wireless, which is a small chain of stores selling cellular wireless phones and a service center. Familia employees are not unionized at this time. However, employees are unhappy with salary, benefits, and the fact that the store is open until 1 a.m. to attract the nighttime club crowd.

Candice previously worked for the Paper Coating Company (PCC), which manufactured paper coating adhesives. This type of paper is often used in greeting cards. PCC was a unionized company. The employees voted in the IBEW (International Brotherhood of Electrical Workers) to represent their 500 employees. The management team at PCC then had to bargain with the union on hours, wages, vacation time, insurance, and safety practices.[1]

Thus, Candice had the opportunity to observe one company that had a unionized workforce and one company that did not have to worry about bargaining with a union.

She noted that employees at PCC had to pay dues to be in the union. The only way for the union to survive is to have its members pay some of their wages (dues) to the union to cover union expenses. Thus, not having a union or dues at Familia Wireless helps employees save money.

On the other hand, she did notice that employees at PCC were threatened with discharge or layoff and that the union fought to protect their jobs. So, it was nice to have union representation when management thought a worker's job performance was not up to standards.

Still, Candice thought the key to deciding to have a union shop was based on the quality of the management team. If there was a good management team in place at your company, then you wouldn't need union representation. You were already being treated and compensated fairly.

However, if the management team was unfair in providing the correct wages, benefits, and working conditions, then a union was a good idea since it could bargain for improvement in these areas.

Candice felt she had a unique view from her spot in HR in both companies. She found that employees of PCC didn't really mind their union dues since the money was automatically deducted from their paycheck. Of course, employees knew (or should have known) they were paying union dues.

Candice worried that if PCC decided to close the company the union would not be overly helpful. She assumed PCC would give the employees the 60 days' notice required by the Worker Adjustment and Retraining Notification Act (WARN). PCC could also offer job retraining at the local community college. But, when PCC wanted to close the company, there wasn't much the union really could do to help employees. Candice's father was an IBEW union member because he worked for AT&T. When AT&T wanted to close his AT&T office in Springfield, Massachusetts, and consolidate offices into a single location in Utah, he was asked to move to Utah or have his employment terminated.

Candice had always heard of violent times in the history of management and unions. Just recently, Candice had heard of Verizon employees who went on strike in 2011 when Verizon tried to freeze pensions for current workers, offer fewer sick days, and put an end to all job security provisions. A major area of concern for the employees was the difference in unionization in the economy; unionization is high in the old landline corded telephone business, but the new wireless cellular business is mostly nonunionized. Employees went on strike for 2 weeks, and many deeply felt the loss of their paychecks during the difficult economy. Verizon, however, received a bad reputation because service was hindered for those 2 weeks.[2]

Chapter Questions

1. What law requires companies to provide employees 60 days' notice if they are going to close?

2. Why would employees want to pay dues to have a union?

3. Do employees need a union if the management team is qualified to do a good job on its own?

4. What is the role of human resources if a company does have a union?

5. Do you think Familia Wireless will unionize?

Case 10.2. Managing Conflicts: How Can HR Help With Angry Employees?

Unfortunately, when two or more people work together for long periods of time, some level of conflict will emerge. *Functional conflict* is a level of conflict that actually helps each employee improve his or her overall performance. However, finding this beneficial level is not an easy task. Too little conflict, and employees can become complacent. Too high levels of conflict can create dysfunction that interferes with workplace performance. A good manager will learn to tweak the office atmosphere to find the proper level of conflict.

During times of conflict, a good manager will also find the conflict management style that works for him or her or will change styles based upon the type of conflict. At times the manager might use an avoiding, accommodating, forcing, negotiating, or collaborative conflict management style. *Avoiding* a conflict is a passive style and often leads to lose-lose situations since both sides lose when resolution of the conflict is not likely. An *accommodating* conflict style means you passively let the other side win the conflict and implement its solution. A *forcing* conflict style uses aggressive behavior, such as authority, to threaten, intimidate, and call for majority rule when you know you have the vote in your favor. *Negotiating* requires finding a compromise that attempts to resolve the conflict through a give-and-take of the issues involved until a solution is found. Last, a *collaborative* style requires working with the other party in the conflict and finding an acceptable solution.

Unfortunately, managers will find it difficult to keep dysfunctional conflict from entering their workplace. Brian Hoffman started his own appliance store designed to provide builders with washers, dryers, refrigerators, and other appliances for a newly built homes. His business grew to include selling appliances to the consumer market through 10 retail outlets. Brian worked out of the main headquarters in Windsor. The human resources, accounting, and marketing departments were also placed at the headquarters.

Brian heard that two workers in his West Hampton store were arguing on the retail floor in front of customers. He sent two HR employees to investigate the problem. It turned out that the two employees had a long-standing problem about who would receive customers as they entered the store. Since the retail employees worked on commission, they both wanted to help customers and fought for them as they entered the store. This was obviously an aggressive form of conflict that was resulting in You Lose, I Win.

Brian asked his HR department to develop a program with which too high a level of conflict could be resolved. Avoiding the problem did not seem like a good solution since the problem was occurring at the point of greeting and helping customers. He also didn't want to force a solution onto the two employees. Ultimately, he wanted to develop a collaborative solution where both parties would like the outcome.

HR decided to look at compensation solutions within a similar setting—selling automobiles. As a growing appliance supplier, Brian's company needed to establish some rules and policies that weren't needed when it was a small business. HR found that car dealerships used a rotating process when customers arrived. Each salesperson would take the next customer as he or she arrived. If more customers arrived at once than could be handled, then all sales personnel would do their best to handle the overflow evenly.

HR also advised Brian to review the compensation system. A compensation system based on salary instead of commission would also lessen the rivalry between salespeople.

Fortunately, the new method of greeting customers was accepted by all retail floor salespeople. The new compensation system based on salary versus commission was being further evaluated.

Brian was satisfied with the results in the employee conflict situation. However, he was concerned about future conflict situations. For example, it was becoming more likely that his growing business would have to discharge employees for not performing up to expectations. Was HR up to the task of processing employees out of the company? Would those employees become violent? HR plays a support role in these serious conflicts: HR can help improve communication between the manager and the employee. HR can be a witness to the confrontation between the two parties. HR can help the employee calm down and return peacefully to the job while looking into the issue. Otherwise, HR can call security or police to help control the disturbed employee.[3]

Brian asked HR to create a program to reduce workplace stress. He wanted to avoid high-level conflict situations before they occurred. Brian also had the realization that his little business was no longer little. There were employees in his business he had never met. While he was busy selling and ordering appliances, HR was busy hiring new employees. He decided to spend more time with HR before he built any new retail sites.

Case Questions

1. Is all conflict bad?

2. What would be the difference between a forcing style and a collaborative style to resolve a conflict?

3. What is the role of HR in resolving workplace conflicts among employees?

4. What is the role of HR in cases with a potentially violent employee?

5. How can HR use the Conflict Resolution Model?

Notes

1. Rowe, Randy Hicks, "What Challenges Do Unions Pose for Human Resource Management?" *Houston Chronicle: Small Business*, http://smallbusiness.chron.com/challenges-unions-pose-human-resource-management-69221.html.

2. Greenhouse, Steven, "Verizon Workers Plan to End Strike, Agreeing to Revive Talks Toward a Contract," *The New York Times*, August 20, 2011, http://www.nytimes.com/2011/08/21/technology/verizon-workers-end-strike-though-without-new-contract.html?_r=0.

3. Maurer, Roy, "When and How Should HR Step Into Violent Situations?" *Society for Human Resource Management*, May 25, 2015, http://www.shrm.org/hrdisciplines/safetysecurity/articles/pages/hr-violent-situations.aspx.

COMPENSATING

PART IV

Compensation Management

Case 11.1. Compensation Management: How Does Wage Compression and Pay Secrecy Affect Employee Motivation?

Marie was the vice-president of human resources for Envelope City, which is a small manufacturing company that makes envelopes for the business market. The company has been in existence for almost 100 years. But there are some problems that can occur with being such an old business. For example, the organizational philosophy on wage compensation most likely was set many years ago when the economic, technological, and social conditions of the country were much different than they are today.

There are seven basic issues that make up the organizational philosophy on compensation. First, Envelope City has to make an honest assessment of how much it can afford and is willing to pay its employees. Second, Envelope has to decide what type of compensation (base pay, wage add-ons, incentives, and benefits) it wants to offer. Third, Envelope has to decide if compensation will be based on loyalty/tenure or if employees will receive raises based on the quality of their work performance. Fourth, a decision needs to be made whether compensation will be based upon a competency-based system that involves the individual's level of knowledge in a particular area or based on the individual skills the person brings to work. Fifth, Envelope needs to decide to pay employees at, above, or below wage levels that workers are receiving at area competitors. Sixth, Envelope has to decide if it is going to allow wage compression to occur between new and long-term employees. Last, Envelope has to decide if pay secrecy (which means employees will not be aware of what each of them is actually paid) will be used within the company.

Interestingly enough, Envelope City found that the last two issues—wage compression and pay secrecy—caused some problems at the company. Wage compression, in particular, is a major problem. Wage compression occurs when new employees require higher starting pay than the historical norm, causing a narrowing of the pay gap between experienced and new employees. The result is that new employees are paid more than longtime employees who are equally talented and at the same level in the organization, regardless of their many years of experience with the company.

Marie experienced a form of wage compression as a teenager when she worked at a fast food restaurant. At the time, back in the 1980s, she had worked hard at a minimum wage of $1.60 per hour. She worked hard for 2 years to earn a dime raise. However, shortly thereafter the minimum wage was increased to $3.20 per hour. Marie lost her dime wage increase for good performance—she made only the minimum of $3.20 per hour.

As a young adult in her twenties, Marie went to work for an oil company and gained 5 years of experience in a human resources department. She then switched jobs to work as the vice-president of human resources at Envelope City. She negotiated a good contract that doubled her salary. However, her salary leap-frogged the other vice-presidents at Envelope City. If her salary was disclosed to the other vice-presidents, they would be very upset to know she was being paid as much or more than the more experienced VPs who had worked at Envelope for many years.

Marie did not intend to create a situation where wage compression was going to be a problem for her new HR department at Envelope City. She felt that the result of her new employee contract (and other similar new employee contracts) was an unintended consequence of Envelope City trying to be a more aggressive employer and to pay new employees a competitive salary compared to the company's competitors.

Another disadvantage of salary compression occurs when lower-level, nonmanagement employees are paid as much, or more, than those in managerial positions.[1] This situation can quickly demotivate key managers.

The only good news about wage compression is that employees often keep their own pay a secret. They are often afraid to compare salaries against each other in case they find that they make less salary than their colleagues.

In 2010, nearly half of all workers were contractually required or encouraged to not talk about their pay level with colleagues.[2] On April 8, 2014, President Obama signed an executive order prohibiting federal contractors, subcontractors, and federally assisted construction contractors from discriminating against employees or applicants who ask other employees about their compensation.

However, pay secrecy might also be one of the reasons that women are paid only 77 cents on the dollar that men make in the same job. Organizations might use pay secrecy to make it difficult for women to compare their salaries with men in similar positions.

Case Question

1. Why does wage compression occur in organizations?

2. How can pay secrecy affect employee motivation?

3. Have you experienced wage compression in your career?

4. Have you experienced pay secrecy?

5. Does President Obama's executive order impact employees at private companies such as Envelope City?

Case 11.2. Trends and Issues in HRM: What Motivates Employees at Work? Expectations or Equity?

Edwidge was thrilled to get a new job at Stubbub soon after she graduated from college with a 4-year degree in management. She was quickly thrown into the position of customer sales and service, selling tickets to sporting events and concerts. After a few months, Edwidge was still in customer service and wondered what her future looked like at Stubbub. She was concerned that she was working very hard but wasn't receiving a salary increase for all her efforts.

This was the first time in Edwidge's life that she wondered why people go to work. Edwidge liked to compare herself to other employees and to figure out whether she was being treated equally. She noticed that all the new employees she started with were working in customer sales and service.

Edwidge decided to look at a few motivation theories to see if they could help her understand her job expectations. Victor Vroom proposed the expectancy theory in 1964 as it applies to motivation. *Expectancy theory* states that Edwidge's motivation is an outcome of how much an individual wants a reward (*valence*). Edwidge assesses the likelihood that her effort will lead to expected performance (*expectancy*) and the belief that the performance will lead to reward (*instrumentality*). Expectancy is Edwidge's faith that better efforts will result in better performance and rewards.[3]

Edwidge next looked at *equity theory,* which was developed by John Stacey Adams in 1963. Adams proposes that Edwidge will be demotivated if she feels her inputs are greater than the outputs she receives. If this happens, Edwidge might respond by being demotivated, reducing her effort, and becoming an unhappy employee.[4]

Edwidge also researched the concept of comparable worth. *Comparable worth* is similar pay for similar work. The concept of comparable worth holds that, if Edwidge can compare her job, skills, responsibilities, and efforts with that of another man or woman, and they are similar, then she should be paid a similar wage. This makes the concept of comparable worth much broader than just equal pay for equal work. The key to similar worth, from a legal standpoint, is to determine the value of a job while also taking into account the supply and demand for a particular job.

One factor in the compensation system at Stubbub also caught Edwidge's attention while doing her research. She detected that pay secrecy was the normal practice at work. She really didn't know what the other employees were getting paid since this information was heavily guarded. Edwidge thought protecting employee salaries was the correct approach for companies to take, but it did make it hard to compare her pay against other employees.

Case Questions

1. Do you think the expectancy theory is correct in explaining what makes Edwidge happy? Explain why or why not.

2. Do you think the equity theory does a better job than the expectancy theory

of explaining what makes employees happy?

3. If you worked in human resources, how would you use positive reinforcement to support employee development?

4. How does pay secrecy make it hard to accept the equity theory?

5. How would Edwidge apply comparable worth to her work situation?

Notes

1. Kochanski, Jim, and Yelena Stiles, "Put a Lid on Salary Compression Before It Boils Over," *Society for Human Resource Management*, July 19, 2013, http://www.shrm.org/hrdisciplines/ compensation/articles/pages/salary-compression-lid.aspx.
2. Women's Bureau, "Fact Sheet," U.S. Department of Labor Women's Bureau, August 2014, http://www.dol.gov/wb/media/pay_secrecy.pdf.
3. http://www.yourcoach.be/en/employee-motivation-theories/vroom-expectancy-motiva tion-theory.php.
4. https://www.mindtools.com/pages/article/newLDR_96.htm.

12

Incentive Pay

Case 12.1. Executive Compensation: New Developments in Executive Compensation

Human resources leaders and compensation experts will always need to attract talented managers to their corporations. However, newer laws are in place to help rein in large executive salaries.

Sarbanes-Oxley (SOX) in 2002 has allowed the Securities and Exchange Commission (SEC) to "claw back" executive pay and stock awards retroactively. SOX has mandatory reporting requirements of all company perks, jets, country club memberships, and so on.[1]

The Dodd-Frank Wall Street Reform and Consumer Protection Act of 2010 was signed into federal law by President Barack Obama on July 21, 2010. Commonly known as the Dodd-Frank, it requires that a public company present to its shareholders a plan to approve compensation, and "enhanced compensation" must be disclosed to the SEC. The goal is to monitor executive compensation by making sure executives are meeting performance-based goals.

The Dodd-Frank Section 953 requires additional disclosure about certain compensation matters, including pay-for-performance and the ratio between the CEO's total compensation and the median total compensation for all other company employees.[2]

SOX and Dodd-Frank are very large laws that HR people might not be able to follow on a daily basis. However, since the recession of 2008, there has been much more attention paid to the large salaries executives receive.

Most large salaries come in the form of stock and stock options in the company. CEOs are rewarded for their performance by receiving these stock options. For example, CEO Larry Ellison of Oracle was paid $96 million in 2012 and $77 million in 2013 (he declined a performance bonus and took $1 in salary).

However, a study by professors found that, the more CEOs got paid, the worse their companies did.[3] One conclusion was that the CEOs became overconfident in their abilities and made poor decisions. Another conclusion might be that they lost their focus and motivation and found other pursuits outside the company to follow. For example, Ellison is very active and a big supporter of yacht racing.

The clawback issue is still being pursued in 2015 as part of Dodd-Frank. The SEC voted to propose a rule that would require exchanges to establish standards for revoking executive bonuses when companies restate earnings or make accounting errors leading to the restatement of earnings, regardless of the executive's fault.[4] The clawback window would extend for 3 years after the bonus was given.

There is also a call for improving the Sarbanes-Oxley legislation since it has been more than 10 years since the regulation has been established. BoardProspects is an online professional community dedicated to building better boards of directors for private, public, and nonprofit organizations. Mark Rogers, the founder and chief executive, posts that the real problem with executive compensation starts with the board of directors. He points at the collapse of Enron as a failure of the board of directors. The board didn't safeguard Enron shareholders and contributed to the collapse of the seventh largest public company in the United States. The board allowed Enron to engage in high-risk accounting, inappropriate conflict of interest transactions, extensive undisclosed off-the-books activities, and excessive executive compensation. Rogers claims that executive pay would be more reasonable if there were term limits on how long a person can serve on a board, limits on the number of boards a person can sit on at one time, and requirements for continuing education on governance as part of his or her training.[5]

Case Questions

1. What is a clawback process in regard to executive compensation?

2. How do the newer laws impact the job of the HR person or compensation expert?

3. Why is the Dodd-Frank legislation so important to executive compensation?

4. Why is Sarbanes-Oxley an important part of HR?

5. What is the role of the board of directors in setting executive pay?

Case 12.2. Trends and Issues in HRM: The Giving Praise Model in Action

The first time David Shaker went to work and was paid was when he was 18 years old. Although David did jobs such as raking leaves and shoveling snow, he was more focused on playing sports than getting a part-time job. During his first year of college, he found his first real job at a McDonald's. The part-time job at McDonald's taught David almost everything he learned about business, and he has used it throughout the rest of his life.

One such learning lesson at McDonald's was in regard to compensation and incentive pay. Individual incentives reinforce performance with a reward that is significant to the person. At 18 years old, David was very happy with a minimum wage of $1.65 and the benefit of a free meal for each shift he worked. Since David was evaluated on his personal performance at the restaurant, it was pretty easy for his manager Naino Leo to evaluate the quality, cleanliness, and service David provided to customers. Plus, it was fairly easy to evaluate David since his job had a distinct outcome (the quality and appearance of the cooked hamburger).

After David graduated from college in 1982, he took a marketing position with the old AT&T. David was evaluated on the performance of the entire group of marketers and their ability to sell expensive telephone systems to business customers. Group incentives provide reinforcement for the actions of more than one individual within the organization. The group evaluation at AT&T did promote teamwork because the employees in David's area had to work together to earn their bonus. Most of the team members were loyal and trusted each other to complete the sales. However, the problem with teamwork at AT&T was that a few employees played the social loafer role. That meant that they didn't work nearly as hard and made fewer sales to customers. These social loafers still expected to share in the bonus each employee would get if the team met or went beyond their sales goal. A bonus is a lump sum payment, typically given to an individual at the end of a time period. Like all employees, David was happy to get a "holiday bonus."

David's next step in his career path led him to Monarch Insurance, where he learned all about the strengths and weaknesses of commission-based sales. A *commission* is a payment typically provided to a salesperson for selling an item to a customer, usually calculated as a percentage of the price of the item sold. In David's case, he sold insurance policies to employees at other companies as part of the benefit those employees were offered. Thus, if David sold an employee from Company ABC an insurance policy to protect his family in case of his death, then David would earn a commission. Many salespeople are paid on a straight commission, meaning that they get paid only if they sell an item. In David's case, he was paid a lower base salary, which was supplemented by commissions on his sales. David felt his salary plus commission compensation structure was implemented properly, and he enjoyed the motivation to increase his paycheck by making more sales. It was important for David to treat customers properly (as he was trained at McDonald's), even if he made a smaller commission. He would rather see that the customers got the correct life insurance policy. Commission sales can motivate salespeople to want to earn the highest commission possible—even if it means that customers buy more product than they actually need.

David felt fortunate that he never worked under a piecework or piece-rate plan. However, he once took a tour of a toy factory, which was under a piece-rate plan, and he watched the employees sorting pieces to include in a 72-piece set. The employees working around the machine were quite calm and peaceful. They just kept inserting bricks, such as the toy head for the person, into the set. When asked, the employees said they were paid for each set of products that was made to the expected quality and specifications. The employees also noted that they enjoyed job rotation and would exchange seats around the machine and belts. That would allow the person to take a different part and insert that part into a different spot in the box. The key for the employees was to work at the proper pace so that they were not working too slowly or too fast. Working too slowly could mean that you weren't making enough of the product. Working too fast could mean that you made mistakes because you didn't have enough time to be careful.

But for all the different compensation plans that David experienced in his different jobs, he was most happy when someone told him he was doing a good job. If the customers said he was doing a good job . . . great! If a manager said he was doing a good job . . . great! If his wife praised him about doing a good job—that was also great!

The *Giving Praise Model* has four steps. The first step is to tell the employee exactly what was done properly. The second step is to tell the employee why the behavior is important. The third step is to allow a moment of silence to give the employee a chance to feel the impact of the praise. The fourth step is to encourage repeat performance so the employee continues to do great work.

Upon reflection, David was always impressed with the praise he received at McDonald's from his boss Naino Leo. Naino gave praise fairly easily, and it didn't cost McDonald's a penny! Managers who use praise will realize that it really works and that employees work even harder to keep up the good work. At times, David did receive praise for finishing his college education, selling telephones for AT&T, or selling an insurance policy. But he also was a little sad that he never quite had the same praise that he had received at 18 years old from his boss Naino.

Case Questions

1. How would you compare hourly wages, having a salary, or being paid by commission?

2. What is the benefit of the Giving Praise Model?

3. Why do companies have a piece-rate system?

4. What is the key step in the praise model?

5. Which type of compensation incentive would you be most likely to receive if you stayed with the same company for 20 years?

Notes

1. Nemer, Kirk D., "New 2015 Developments in Executive Compensation," *Executive Career Insider*, May 28, 2015, https://www.bluesteps.com/blog/executive-compensation-2015.

2. https://www.sec.gov/spotlight/dodd-frank/corporategovernance.shtml.

3. Adams, Susan, "The Highest-Paid CEOs Are the Worst Performers, New Study Says," *Forbes*, June 16, 2014, http://www.forbes.com/sites/susanadams/2014/06/16/the-highest-paid-ceos-are-the-worst-performers-new-study-says/.

4. "SEC Proposes Executive Bonus 'Clawback' Rule," *ABA Banking Journal*, July 1, 2015, http://bankingjournal.aba.com/2015/07/sec-proposes-executive-bonus-clawback-rule/.

5. Rogers, Mark, "Sarbanes-Oxley 10 Years Later: Boards Are Still the Problem," *Forbes*, July 29, 2012.

13

Employee Benefits

Case 13.1. Statutory Benefits: Companies Kicking Your Spouse Off of Your Health Care Plans

Dennis Ferry works for Compatible Technology in its customer service department. Dennis knows he will have to make plenty of decisions when open enrollment for his company health plan, Health New England, rolls around July 1 each year. Dennis's health-care coverage was totally free for employees in 1982 when he was just out of college. That was a long time ago—and health care in the United States has changed dramatically.

Today, companies are looking to save as much money as possible when designing a health-care program. Each employee who signs up for the company health-care program can cost the company between $4,000 and $10,000 a year, depending on the program selected. Of course, it would be nice to think that the companies (and our government) are also trying to make sure we receive the best health care possible.

Dennis's wife, Janice Ferry, is employed by LEGO. Dennis and Janice have three daughters under 10 years old. As a family, they can expect to pay about $300 a month for the plan offered by Compatible Technology. They can also expect a deductible around $2,500 to $4,000. The Compatible health-care plan has a deductible of $2,500, which means the Ferrys will have to pay $2,500 in actual medical costs for pharmaceutical drugs, office visits, hospital stays, and so on before they can expect to receive "free" health service until July 1 rolls around again.

If Dennis worked for UPS, Janice would have to take health-care insurance from her job at LEGO, since she would not be allowed to stay on the Compatible plan. That would happen because UPS informed their employees that their spouses would be dropped from their health-care plan if the spouse can obtain health care at his or her own place of employment.[1] This measure was taken as a reaction to the Affordable Care Act (ACA). UPS expects to save money by avoiding paying the premiums for each person on the plan. These premiums were implemented as part of the ACA.[2]

In Dennis's case, he recently had to decide if he wanted to receive a $3,000 payment from his employer, Compatible Technology, to not take his health-care benefits.

The $3,000 must be used to pay for a spouse's health-care program. Thus, if Dennis didn't take Compatible's health-care plan from Health New England, he would be paid $3,000 to help pay for health-care benefits at LEGO, where his wife works. Proof of the other health-care plan must be provided. In Dennis's case, since his wife Janice worked for LEGO with a generous health-care plan, they decided to take the offer from Compatible for $3,000 and would apply it to a family plan offered by LEGO. This appears to be a positive switch in plans, since even Compatible will be happy that it will not have to pay its portion of Dennis's health-care plan, which would be greater than $3,000.

Case Questions

1. Approximately how much money would a company spend on a health-care plan for Janice as compared to her own cost?

2. What did UPS claim as the reason for dropping spouses from its health-care plans?

3. What decisions does Janice have to make in regard to selecting her health-care plan?

4. At UPS, what would be the result if your spouse was forced to use his or her own company plan?

5. What health-care plan are you covered by at this time? Are you working for a company and have you accepted the company plan? Are you on your parents' plan, which you can be covered on until age 26?

Case 13.2. Trends and Issues in HRM: Managing New Laws Regarding Sick Leave

It might be surprising to know, but there is no general legal requirement that employers give employees sick leave in the United States. While most employers do give employees some paid time off each year to be used for sick leave, the law does not require employers to do so in most circumstances. Since there is no requirement under federal law that employees be given sick leave, there also is no legal requirement that sick leave, if given by an employer, be paid leave.

The following passage is from the U.S. Department of Labor.

Currently, there are no federal legal requirements for paid sick leave. For companies subject to the Family and Medical Leave Act (FMLA), the Act does require unpaid sick leave. FMLA provides for up to 12 weeks of unpaid leave for certain medical situations for either the employee or a member of the employee's immediate family. In many instances paid leave may be substituted for unpaid FMLA leave.

Employees are eligible to take FMLA leave if they have worked for their employer for at least 12 months, and have worked for at least 1,250 hours over the previous 12 months, and work at a location where at least 50 employees are employed by the employer within 75 miles.[3]

An estimated 43 million people nationwide have no paid sick time. Employees without time for sick leave often make up excuses to take time off or try to work when they are sick. Employees also have to figure out what to do when their child is sick and needs to stay home, when they need to go to their own doctor, or when they need to help a sick relative.

However, cities and states are starting to propose and pass laws that provide workers with sick leave time. A city of Pittsburgh councilman has proposed an ordinance that allows employees to earn sick days based upon the number of hours they have worked. The draft legislation allows 30 hours of work to equal 1 hour of sick time. Employees cannot earn more than 72 hours of sick time in a year. Businesses with fewer than 15 employees can limit sick time to 40 hours.[4]

Effective July 1, 2015, the state of Massachusetts passed the Earned Sick Time Law, which provides 1 hour of sick time for 40 hours of work. Earned sick time is paid at the employee's normal rate of pay. Employers that have 11 employees or more must allow their employees to earn and use up to 40 hours of paid sick time per calendar year. Employees working for an employer with fewer than 11 employees can earn up to 40 hours of unpaid sick leave per calendar year. An employee may miss work (1) to care for a physical or mental illness, injury, or medical condition affecting the employee or the employee's child, spouse, parent, or parent of a spouse; (2) to attend routine medical appointments or those of a child, spouse, parent, or parent of a spouse; or (3) to address the effects of domestic violence on the employee or the employee's dependent child.[5]

Six and a half million people in California became eligible for paid sick leave for the first time starting July 1, 2015. The Healthy Workplace Healthy Family Act of 2014 guarantees up to three days of paid sick leave for all California workers who work for 30 or more days within a year of becoming employed. The law will help employees in the retail and fast food industry, since those employees often have young children and often need to take sick time to tend to those children when they are ill.

Overall, as of July 2015, California, Connecticut, Massachusetts, and the District of Columbia, as well as at least 18 cities, have laws mandating paid sick days.[6]

Case Questions

1. Is sick time part of paid time off benefits?

2. Do you believe that employees abuse sick leave by using a "use it or lose it" approach?

3. Does having a sick leave policy help reduce overall stress?

4. Why doesn't a national sick leave law exist?

5. Does the company you (or your relative) work for have a sick leave policy? If so, what is that policy?

Notes

1. Ponder, Crissinda, "Will Company Health Plans Drop Spouses?" *Bankrate.com,* http://www.bankrate.com/finance/insurance/employer-health-plans-drop-spouses.aspx.

2. Greenhouse, Steven, "U.P.S. to End Health Benefits for Spouses of Some Workers," *New York Times,* August 21, 2013.

3. United States Department of Labor, "Work Hours: Sick Leave," http://www.dol.gov/dol/topic/workhours/sickleave.htm.

4. Zullo, Robert, "Pittsburgh Council to Introduce Paid Sick-Leave Legislation," *Pittsburgh Post-Gazette,* July 6, 2015, http://www.post-gazette.com/local/2015/07/06/Council-to-introduce-paid-sick-leave-legislation/stories/201507030268.

5. http://smcattorneys.com/employment-law-update-massachusetts-sick-leave-law/.

6. Karol, Gabrielle, "California Paid Sick Leave Act Goes Into Effect July 1," *USA Today Network,* June 30, 2015.

PROTECTING AND EXPANDING ORGANIZATIONAL REACH

14

Workplace Safety, Health, and Security

Case 14.1. Building a Human Resources Information System While Protecting Health Information From Cyber Attacks

Kendra Lewis was hired right out of college to support the human resources staff at an insurance company in Orange County, California. It took Kendra about a year to become familiar with all the paper forms that were completed by the employees of the insurance company. One day her boss, Sam Cooke, told her they were going to develop a Human Resources Information System (HRIS). Sam had very little idea what was involved in an HRIS; he had only heard about the concept at a conference that he recently attended. So Sam told Kendra to research what was involved in such a system.

Kendra found that the age of technology had created the need to create an HRIS to effectively coordinate everything related to human resources. A modern HRIS would be a software solution that would create a database whereby her human resource department could collect employee information; would create reports and analyses about employee information; would store company-related documents, such as employee handbooks; would track applications and résumés for open positions; and would complete integration with payroll and other company financial software and accounting systems so that employees would be paid properly.[1] A modern HRIS contains information about which benefits an employee selects; status changes, such as promotions at work; and personal information.

To help track applicants and résumés for open positions, a modern HRIS automates the application process by providing a standard application to candidates by way of the Internet. The application and other related documents from the applicant can then be stored on the HRIS. The search committee filling the open position can then review applications online, using a company's Intranet system. Search members can use keyword searches to provide the HR manager with a first cut of suitable applicants for a specific job.

The amount of information flowing through an HRIS regarding protected health information (PHI) is increasing rapidly. Since Kendra's insurance company is growing rapidly, the data will grow accordingly given that the number of employees and their dependents who apply for health care will increase on the company payroll.

Employee privacy regarding health insurance is an important issue when developing an HRIS. Human resource professionals like Kendra will need to be trained in the Health Insurance Portability and Accountability Act of 1996 (HIPAA) Privacy, Security and Breach Notification Rules. As defined by the Office of Civil Rights, the HIPPA Privacy Rule protects the privacy of individually identifiable health information. The HIPAA Security Rule sets national standards for the security of electronically protected health information. The HIPAA Breach Notification Rule requires notification following a breach of unsecured protected health information.[2] Since Kendra and the other HR office personnel will have electronic access to all employee information, the need for following the rules of HIPPA will be increased, since it can be much harder to protect electronic files than a paper file.

HR professionals need to understand that the protected health information (PHI) entrusted to them is to be confidential at all times. Cautious employees are good employees to hire in a human resource department. The need for trusted and confidential employees in HR is critical.

HR should conduct a risk assessment to start the process of protecting the PHI. The assessment can include protective measures already in place and those that are missing. Part of the assessment must include an assessment of third-party suppliers, such as the company that produces the employee checks or the company hired to be the expert at managing the employer-sponsored health-care and retirement programs. Kendra's company uses BBG Health Service Provider to develop the company healthcare program and collect all employee funds related to health insurance. Kendra's company also uses Deluxe Check Writing Services to produce employee checks. Deluxe and BBG are two examples of very important third-party suppliers to the human resources department. Providers such as Deluxe and BBG must ensure the safety of the employee data they use while providing their services.

Kendra found that an HRIS will require many high-tech solutions, such as software selection and updates. *Cyber security* is the use of tools and processes to protect organizational computer systems and networks. Professional and amateur hackers, terrorist organizations, and even some governments are working to break into company computer systems for a variety of reasons. In 2015, two major breaches of U.S. government databases holding personnel records and security-clearance files exposed sensitive information of at least 22.1 million people. Exposed personal information was hacked about federal employees, contractors, their families, and friends. U.S. officials have privately said that the intrusions were traced to the Chinese government.[3]

Although many high-tech solutions will be needed to safeguard employee data, some simple solutions such as strong passwords and changing passwords on a regular basis can help protect the HRIS and PHI. Employees and HR professionals can also be careful not to leave unsecured laptops with employee data in unlocked areas.

Overall, an HRIS will allow the company to reduce its own paper needs, save time, reduce stress, and create a more efficient process of helping employees with their salary and benefits. Kendra proposed to her boss that a committee should be formed so that the system reflects the needs of all the stakeholders of the organization.

Case Questions

1. What are the goals of a human resources information system?

2. In comparison, what is the goal of protected health information?

3. Why do HR professionals need HIPPA training?

4. Why are third-party suppliers a potential security risk?

5. What are some simple solutions to help reduce cyber attacks on PHI?

6. Who should Kendra consider to be members on the committee to develop the HRIS?

Case 14.2. Trends and Issues in HRM: Future Trends in Human Resource Management

Past issues related to HRM will always be important to the future issues in HRM. Topics such as legal issues involving the rights of employees, recruiting employees, matching employees with jobs that fit their skill set, selecting employees, developing and training employees, evaluating the performance of employees, compensating employees, providing employee health-care and retirement benefits, and developing an HRIS to maintain all that information will all need to continue to improve. A growing area of importance to HR is providing workplace safety. Workplace safety is an area that is of great concern; we want our employees to feel secure while performing their jobs. We also want to make sure our employees are healthy so they can perform their jobs and enjoy their lives.

From an HRM perspective, the goal might be to become a more powerful player in the management of the organization. HR would like to be consulted on strategic issues that are often associated with the finance or marketing areas. However, in most companies, HR will always be considered a staff area as compared to the more active line areas, such as marketing or finance. Still, with the increased diversity of our workforce and the changes needed in employee skills, HR will certainly be a very busy area of a company.

HR will be busy with topics such as how to incorporate technology into its functions, how to analyze employee data produced by technology to help make HR decisions, how to use social media to find talented employees, how to increase our understanding of how diversity impacts our workforce, and how to address generational issues in the workplace caused by having up to five generations of people working together.

These issues will certainly impact HR functions at all organizations. Prospective employees will use social media (such as LinkedIn and Facebook) to find job openings.

Prospects will use social networks to develop relationships and a network of people to help find job matches.

Prospective employees will have to be persistent in their search to find the company that is a good match. Employers will find it hard to stay competitive in their industries as technology changes the workplace. For example, Hallmark Cards in Enfield, Connecticut, will lay off 570 employees in 2016 and move its distribution center to a single location in Liberty, Missouri.[4] Only 400 employees were offered in Missouri. Human resources will have to be involved in processing the employees either to work in Missouri, to be retrained to work in a new industry, to prepare for an early retirement, or to be helped through the unemployment process.

People will have to acquire skills that are needed by employers. Increasingly, companies will contract out to training organizations that specifically train employees in skills such as computer programming. People will often train themselves for free by completing massive open online courses (MOOCs) to learn specific skills. The millennial group will use their desire to learn and use technology to enter companies at the same time as baby boomers exit companies and head into retirement.

The development of HRIS using massive computer power will increasingly replace the paperwork typically associated with human resources. The only way to avoid being eliminated by the computer revolution is to join it by making sure each one of us is computer educated in our own career.

A great concern is the safety, health, and security of our workers while on the job. The following workplace incidents, unfortunately, occurred with the past few months of writing this text. A newscaster and her cameraman were killed by a bitter ex-television reporter 2 years after he was fired.[5] A student killed nine people when he attacked a building at Umpqua Community College in Roseburg, Oregon.[6] Fourteen people were killed and 22 injured in a workplace massacre at the Inland Regional Center in San Bernardino, California.[7]

People can become aware of workplace safety issues much faster than in the past. The popularity of social media sites, such as Facebook and Twitter, have allowed people to be aware of situations while they are happening. Social media can assist companies in dealing with a situation where employees need information quickly and accurately. Alert systems can provide immediate warnings to all people signed up to receive alerts.

Violence in the workplace requires HRM to be proactive and to have policies and procedures in place in case a violent situation does occur. A written policy addressing workplace violence is the best preventive policy. It is important for HR people to take action quickly and to address any individuals at work who show potential violent behaviors and actions.

Organizations need to have a formal grievance process at work to allow frustrated employees to air their complaints. The process will take time to develop, and it most likely will involve many steps, since a well-written policy makes sure the employee meets with all parties involved before reaching a formal grievance hearing. Demotions, firing, and layoffs need to be handled in a professional manner and in all cases should include helping the employee find a new place of employment that might be a better fit for his or her talents.

Case Questions

1. Will HR become more, less, or stay the same in regard to its importance within companies?

2. What is the role of technology in the future of human resources?

3. What are some areas of HR that will be important in the future of HR?

4. What other areas of HR do you envision as being important in the future of HR?

5. Research workplace violence that has happened in your own local area within the last year.

Notes

1. http://humanresources.about.com/od/glossaryh/a/hris.htm.

2. http://www.hhs.gov/ocr/privacy/.

3. Nakashima, Ellen, "Hacks of OPM Databases Compromised 22.1 Million People, Federal Authorities Say," *The Washington Post*, July 9, 2015.

4. Porter, Mikaela, and Mara Lee, "Hallmark to Close Enfield Warehouse, Eliminate 570 Jobs," *Hartford Courant*, July 7, 2015, http://www.courant.com/business/hc-enfield-hallmark-warehouse-close-20150707-story.html.

5. Sandoval, Edgar, Jason Silverstein, and Larry McShane, "TV News Reporter, Cameraman Are Fatally Shot During Live Broadcast in Virginia; Suspected Shooter Posts Video of Attack, Then Kills Himself," *New York Daily News,* August 27, 2015.

6. Turkewitz, Julie, "Oregon Gunman Smiled, Then Fired, Student Says," *New York Times.com*, October 9, 2015.

7. Sanchez, Ray, Michael Martinez, and Doug Criss, "'Pray for Us': Calls, Texts Relay Horror of California Mass Shooting," *CNN.com*, December 2, 2015.

15

Organizational Ethics, Sustainability, and Social Responsibility

Case 15.1. Corporate Social Responsibility (CSR): Can Human Resources Help Companies Develop a CSR Program?

One of the hotter topics in business in the last 10 years has been corporate social responsibility (CSR). *CSR* means taking all stakeholders into account. All stakeholders means all—not just shareholders or executives. The business case for CSR is based on the ability of the organization to help or harm various stakeholder groups and to identify, of those stakeholder groups, which ones help or harm the company. Each stakeholder group has different, and sometimes competing, interests. The organization must balance these social responsibilities among all the groups in order to succeed.

A CSR program recognizes that organizations have a duty to all stakeholders to operate in a manner that takes each of their needs into account. It signifies an attempt by organizations to be more aware of and to develop programs to create a *triple P concept*—people, planet, and profits. The goal is to save the planet, help people live a better lives, and still produce a profit for the shareholders, owners, and employees to share.

HR can play a role in helping organizations and employees be more CSR oriented. So far, HR hasn't been active enough in this area. But HR can make sure that management is ethically oriented. HR can make sure employees are ethically oriented by providing training and development on CSR. HR can make sure that ethics is adhered to at the board level of the company.[1]

Ethics is commonly understood to include morals, values, beliefs, and principles. An employee with these characteristics will have personal integrity and be known as a trustworthy person. An ethical employee can be expected to want to help a company develop a CSR program.

In terms of the planet, HR can teach employees to think about sustainable issues. Employees look for improvements in their work areas. They can use suppliers that employ sustainable measures, such as paper packaging produced from recycled paper or renewable forests. Businesses and their employees can lower the use of environmentally damaging chemicals in the production of their products. Employees can learn to reduce or reuse waste products.

In regard to people, HR can help employees take care of their health by promoting the use of health-care benefits, such as reimbursement for membership to health-care clubs. Or HR can help employees find a better balance between work and family life.

However, the goal remains being a profitable business. Even a nonprofit business needs to break even to ensure staying in operation. The Triple P concept looks for ways to improve the environment, help employees, and yet still be profitable.

The American economist Milton Friedman felt that using any money to improve the environment, beyond what is required by the government, was not a good use of company finances since it would reduce overall profits.[2] Accordingly, Friedman did not support the widespread use of CSR. He felt a company should do only what it legally needed to do as required by the law.

However, research by Edward Freeman resulted in a different view. Freeman's *stakeholder theory* called for managers to create value for customers, suppliers, employees, communities, and shareholders. Freeman took a much broader view on creating value for everyone instead of just making profits for shareholders.[3] Thus, Freeman would support the concept of CSR and the idea that a company should go beyond its legal requirements and help the people, planet, and profits all at the same time.

Since 2012, Apple Computers has faced troubles in regard to its supplier Foxconn in Taiwan. Foxconn has 1.2 million employees who make Apple's very profitable iPads, iPhones, and other high-tech products. However, the employees work under extreme conditions to ensure that Apple products are consistently produced at a high quality.[4] The repetition of the work has led many of the employees to feel depressed, and some employees have tried to commit suicide. Foxconn has installed nets around the roof of the company to prevent jumping off the building.[5]

Still, just because Apple has trouble with a supplier doesn't automatically make it an unethical company. Nike had a very similar problem with its suppliers in the 1990s. Nike footwear was made in sweatshop conditions in Indonesia. Nikes were made by workers who were paid low wages and experienced poor working conditions.[6] Nike was also accused of using children to make its footwear. Nike did its own research and found that the poor working conditions were real and needed to be corrected. The company has spent the last decade trying to publish where its footwear is produced and trying to train the managers in those locations not to use hurtful tactics (such as forcing workers to stay outside in the blazing sun after failing to reach their goal of 60 pairs of shoes on time).[7] Nike has joined the Fair Labor Association, a group that includes other footwear and clothing makers, nongovernment organizations (NGOs), and universities, which conducts independent audits designed to improve standards across the industry.

Case Questions

1. How do Milton Friedman and Edward Freeman differ on their views of an organization's role in corporate social responsibility?

2. Has HR been active enough in CSR?

3. What can HR do to promote CSR in an organization?

4. How can HR help the planet?

5. Why did Apple have trouble with Foxconn?

Case 15.2. Equal Opportunity, Diversity, and Multiple Generations at Work Together

Title VII of the Civil Rights Act of 1964 was enacted to stop discrimination based on race, color, sex, national origin, and religion. In later years, the meaning of diversity expanded to include individuals with disabilities, workers aged 40 years and over, and veterans.[8] Today, workplace diversity includes differences attributed to generation, culture, and lifestyles.

Employee diversity will continue to grow, and we will have to become better at managing that diversity than we have in the past. To exclude a qualified person because that individual is different in some way is counterproductive to business success. Managing diversity is becoming critical in all organizations and in all industries. We have to continue to get better at the HRM task in order to engage all our future employees.

Generational differences are one of the latest and most interesting areas of potential differences. Workplaces often have four or five different generations working together. These generations are labeled Traditionalist (born 1922–1945), Baby Boomers (born 1946–1964), Generation X (born 1965–1980), and Generation Y (born 1980–1994), also known as the Millennial Generation or Generation Next.[9]

Traditionalists tend to work late and on weekends. They grew up in a time when wives stayed at home and didn't work. They are loyal employees and expect to be paid fairly well. Changing jobs did not occur often, since that meant something was not going well.

Baby Boomers were born in an era of general affluence. Many grew up in a household with a single parent working. Women are often as educated as men. Boomers can be driven to succeed.

Gen Xers are often children who lived with two working parents. They tend to be individualistic, confident, and self-reliant. They believe that balancing family life and work life is most important. Xers are the first generation to feel comfortable with technology and diversity.

Millennials are very knowledgeable about technology. They are also very understanding of diversity and expressing personal lifestyle choices. They are able to multitask and like to work at their own pace.[10]

Today's business environment is the first one in which five generations of people are likely to be working at the same time. The differences in age could create conflict between the younger and older employees. However, the differences between employee ages should be cherished and used as a source of information to help sell company products. Managing older workers will be important as younger people take over the leadership role in all organizations.[11]

Older employees (such as Traditionalists and Baby Boomers) are often the mentors for teaching younger (Gen X and Y) employees. Older workers can teach younger workers about the culture of the company and how things normally get done.

However, Gen X and Y employees have been born in the technology era. That being so, the younger employees can teach older employees about topics such as social media marketing techniques. So younger employees can become reverse mentors and teach the older employees how to better use technology in the workplace.

Case Questions

1. What are the traditional areas of discrimination the human resources department normally helps to resolve?

2. How do equal opportunity, diversity, and generational issues intersect?

3. What generation do you belong to? Do the characteristics describe yourself?

4. What differences do you experience between yourself and a coworker (or teacher) from a different generation?

5. What potential discrimination issues do you think exist between employees of different generations?

Notes

1. Higginbottom, Karen, "Why HR Needs to Take a Leadership Role in CSR," *Forbes,* January 6, 2006.

2. Friedman, Milton, "The Social Responsibility of Business Is to Increase Its Profits," *The New York Times Magazine,* September 13, 1970.

3. Freeman, Edward, *Strategic Management* (Boston, MA: Pitman, 1984).

4. Leach, Anna, "Foxconn Is World's 10th Largest Employer: 1.2 Million Employees," *The Register,* March 20, 2012.

5. Myers, Connor, "Corporate Social Responsibility in the Consumer Electronics Industry: A Case Study of Apple Inc.," Georgetown University, http://lwp.georgetown.edu/wp-content/uploads/Connor-Myers.pdf.

6. Nisen, Max, "How Nike Solved Its Sweatshop Problem," *Business Insider.com,* May 9, 2013.

7. Teather, David, "Nike Lists Abuses at Asian Factories," *The Guardian,* April 14, 2005.

8. Mayhew, Ruth, "What Are an Employer's Responsibilities for Diversity in the Workplace?" *Houston Chronicle: Small Business,* http://smallbusiness.chron.com/employers-responsibilities-diversity-workplace-10417.html.

9. http://www.valueoptions.com/spotlight_YIW/gen_y.htm.

10. Jerome, Alicia, and Michael Scales, "Millennials in the Workforce: Gen Y Workplace Strategies for the Next Century," *e-Journal of Social & Behavioural Research in Business* 5, no. 1 (2014): 1–12.

11. Hoving, Allan, "Managing Older Workers," *Human Resources IQ.com,* October 24, 2013.

16

Global Issues for Human Resource Managers

Case 16.1. Globalization of Business and HRM: Should Your Marketing Director Become an Expatriate?

Daniel had a successful career in marketing for IToys Corporation in New York. Daniel's career has been an exciting journey through IToys, which is the fastest growing toy business in the United States. However, IToys had plans to enter the global marketplace, and human resources called Daniel with an offer to manage the new office in England for the next 3 years. Daniel's career would be kicked up a notch by being the director of marketing for the entire United Kingdom.

HR determined that Daniel had many of the Big 5 personality traits (extroversion, openness to new experiences, conscientiousness, agreeableness, and not being neurotic) that would help him to be successful running IToys in different countries. Daniel is an extrovert; he is outgoing, makes new friends, and builds relationships easily. Some evidence shows that being an extrovert, open to learning about new international cultures and experiences, and working well with new people will help him adjust to a different culture.[1]

Although Daniel was surprised about the offer to take an assignment in England, he knew that he was open to new experiences. Before working at IToys, Daniel spent plenty of time in Europe at trade shows demonstrating toys for his previous employer. The problem was that Daniel had a wife, Hannah, and three children between the ages of 5 and 10. Daniel had a tough decision to make in regard to uprooting his family and moving them all the way to England. Hannah had been a great supporter of her husband for the last 5 years. She had moved up and down the East Coast (New Jersey, Rhode Island, Pennsylvania, and Massachusetts) in support of Daniel. Daniel had to consider the impact on his wife since she would be thrown into a new country with no friends. Daniel's children would have to start school in a strange country.

Still, Daniel and Hannah decided to become expatriates, and they accepted the new position in England. An *expatriate* is an employee who leaves his or her home country to go to work in another country. Many decisions have to be made since the "expat" is usually in another country for about 3 years. One decision that would have to be made was in regard to schooling for their children. Daniel and Hannah decided that their children would attend the American School and attend classes with the children of other American executives.

Human resources at IToys offered various services to help Daniel make the move to England. HR explained that his home in New York would be paid for by the company while he was away for 3 years. HR would provide training on cultural issues such as language (a lesser problem in this case due to English being spoken in both countries). HR would also process Daniel's pay so he would be paid in U.S. dollars, which he could then transfer to English pounds or euros. HR would be the contact point for Daniel throughout his international journey.

Daniel and Hannah ended up enjoying their 3 years of marketing IToys in England. Hannah was an integral piece of the puzzle. She became an important person in the expat community. While Daniel was busy setting up new retail accounts for IToys to sell their product lines, Hannah was busy taking care of the children and making sure they adjusted to a new set of friends. Hannah also made trips back to the United States to attend to elderly family members or to attend important family celebrations. IToys allows its expats to return to their home country once a year.

It is important for the expats to be compensated above normal to help alleviate the extra costs of living overseas. The executives and their families move to another country and experience the international lifestyle. However, they still need to be part of their family back in their home country, which requires extra money for travel expenses.

Other issues, besides language, that can cause problems with an overseas job include determining whom the person reports to in the host country versus the home country, who appraises the expat in regard to performance, whether there will be a mentor in the host country to help train Daniel, and what support will be available from human resources during and after the assignment is complete.

After 3 years, Daniel was offered the chance to start up a new division of IToys in Brazil. Being in Brazil would bring them to another expat community. However, this time they could experience more culture shock, as Portuguese is the primary language of 99 percent of the people in Brazil. Daniel would need to have more cultural training since doing business in Brazil would be quite different than it was in England. Still, Daniel and his family thrived in England, so they are experienced expats. They certainly appear to be flexible, and they may enjoy learning more about the Brazilian culture.

Case Questions

1. What does it mean to be an expatriate?

2. What would it have meant to Daniel's career if he had declined the position in England?

3. Why was Hannah such an important part of the entire expatriate experience?

4. What is the role of human resources in assisting expatriates?

5. How did language play a part of the decision to go to either England or Brazil?

6. Should Daniel take the new job in Brazil?

Case 16.2. Global Staffing: Developing, Staffing, and Managing Global Human Resources—Katya and Her Russian Background

Katya Malkin is proof that we are living in a global village. Companies have to search for talented employees, like Katya, throughout the world. In Katya's case, she was a gifted student while in school in Russia. But she was raised in a very poor home environment. Although she had a lovely mother and father, she lived in a small one-bedroom apartment.

Fortunately, at school Katya excelled at math and science, like many of her fellow Russian-born students. She also spoke English very well. Katya was quite social and interacted very well with teachers and counselors. At 15, Katya was extremely fortunate, and she went to the United States for high school. She lived with a wonderful family in a suburb of Connecticut. She applied and was accepted at a small Catholic College in Danbury, Connecticut.

Katya had 4 wonderful years studying management, marketing, and accounting. She found that large employers were especially interested in hiring her for her degree in accounting.

Katya wrote a senior thesis on how companies hired international students to help give organizations a global view. She found that employers like international students but consider the process of hiring an international student rather complex. Understanding the American immigration process is often stressful and confusing because there are many different categories of visas. The eligibility requirements are constantly changing, which makes the process even harder to follow.[2]

On the positive side, international students like Katya have already shown that they can leave their home country and learn the language of a new country, and they show a desire to work in the United States. Katya assumed it would be easy to entice international students to also live as expats in other countries.

The human resources department of a company can help employees renew a visa. HR can also help international students become part of the local community, find schools that offer programs for bilingual students, and make spouses feel like a part of the company.

A company is only as good as the people who work for it. Employees will be needed to replace people who are retiring from the workforce, who are transferring to another company, or who have passed away. HR has to fill these spots with talented people in every country where their product is sold. Hiring recently graduated international college students can help fill job openings within and outside the United States.

The HR function becomes more complex as companies experience different stages of developing a global organization. HR has to develop HRIS systems that take into account the culture and business practices of every country in which they operate. Still, for those people like Katya who are extroverted, agreeable, and open to new experiences, taking a chance and becoming an expatriate can lead to an exciting life of travel, meeting people from different countries, negotiating deals around the globe, and working for the large global companies in places as diverse as China, Poland, and Israel.

Case Questions

1. What are the advantages of hiring a recently graduated international college student?

2. What are the disadvantages of hiring a recently graduated international college student?

3. What is the impact on HR when hiring an international student?

4. Use the website http://www.reed .co.uk/jobs/human-resources to look for a human resources job in the United Kingdom.

5. Find a job in another country of your choice. You should feel that you would have a good opportunity to be selected for the job.

Notes

1. Lussier, Robert, and John R. Hendon, *Human Resource Management,* 2nd ed. (Thousand Oaks, CA: Sage, 2016).

2. http://www.internationalstudent.com/study_usa/way-of-life/working-in-the-usa/.